THE COUP D'ÉTAT
AGAINST PRESIDENT DONALD J. TRUMP

BY
DAVID MEADE

Copyright 2017 David Meade
All rights reserved

Published by eBookIt.com

ISBN-13: 978-1-4566-2827-7

No part of this book may be reproduced in any form or by any electronic or mechanical means including information storage and retrieval systems, without permission in writing from the author. The only exception is by a reviewer, who may quote short excerpts in a review.

TABLE OF CONTENTS

FOREWORD BY THE AUTHOR 1

THE FALSE NARRATIVES OF OBAMA 3

ILLUMINATI PLANS FOR AMERICA 6

THE SHADOW GOVERNMENT AND JFK 8

DONALD TRUMP'S LIGHTNING WAR AGAINST THE NEW WORLD ORDER 11

MASONIC POWERS 13

THE MANCHURIAN CANDIDATE 14

OBAMA ALMOST PROVOKED THE RUSSIANS 15

DECEPTION BY THE ALPHABET AGENCIES 18

THE CONTRACTORS FOR THE ELITE 20

THE GOALS OF THE NEW WORLD ORDER 21

WAR IN SYRIA 23

BEHOLD, A PALE HORSE 24

CONTROLLING U.S. PRESIDENTS 26

THE COMMITTEE OF 300 28

THE NEWS BEHIND THE NEWS 30

THE SECRETS OF WORLD WAR II 31

THE NEW WORLD ORDER COLLAPSE 35

NEW WORLD ORDER MACHINATIONS FOR A GREAT DEPRESSION 38

RUSSIA ABANDONS THE DOLLAR 42

IS THE LEVIATHAN GAS FIELD THE LARGEST NATURAL GAS FIELD IN THE WORLD? 43

IS GLOBAL ECONOMIC COLLAPSE UNAVOIDABLE? 44

DERIVATIVES PANIC IN GLOBAL MARKETS 46

THE MAINSTAY OF PRECIOUS METALS 48

SEVEN EXPERTS WHO AGREE WITH ME 52

THE PLAN TO OVERTHROW THE U.S. ECONOMY BY THE NWO 54

UNDERSTANDING HISTORICAL COLLAPSES 61

OIL, GEOPOLITICS AND WAR 70

ESSENTIAL KNOWLEDGE 80

EXECUTING A PLAN 86

THE ART OF INTELLIGENCE 100

CHINESE DECEPTION 104

THE END GAME 106

THE COUP D'ÉTAT AGAINST PRESIDENT DONALD J. TRUMP

FOREWORD BY THE AUTHOR

This book will explore the deep background of who is behind operations against our President, how they are funded and lastly, what you can do about it to protect yourself. We'll explore the myriad of Secret Societies and front organizations, and name the people as well. Now listen to this - when all else fails, the deluded New World Order group will attempt to create a global economic crisis. Don't be concerned – this book covers every angle and how you can protect yourself.

Donald Trump is one cool character. I like the way he operates. Let's look at the probable NSA data leak with General Michael Flynn. Flynn allegedly misled Vice President Mike Pence about his conversations with Russia's ambassador to Washington. But as Trump said, he has been treated very poorly. I don't believe he broke the law, and moreover someone like Flynn, former head of the DIA, is an invaluable asset.

He has close to forty years of contacts and intelligence analyst ability. These people are amazingly trained and connected, and he could have done a superlative job for the American people.

This entire situation is part of a failed coup d'état against our President, and it's falling back right on to the perpetrators. These people needless to say were not the sharpest pencils in the box. I'm almost 100% certain they weren't smart enough to use cut-outs or dead drops in their leaks to the reporters. They likely used their cell telephones and email addresses, and if they did, they're as good as indicted right now by a grand jury.

Trump has unleashed the power of the Department of Justice on these people. The FBI will be interviewing the reporters. This is a felony and it is actually treason. I suspect these people are "Obama leftovers."

Now the NSA does an amazing job – but these are rogue elements we are dealing with. However, the NSA should not allow unrestricted access to their people of these data transcripts. 60,000 people have access. It wouldn't be difficult to restrict access. I'm certain the NSA is considering options or else Congress will.

Recommendations have been put forward that the agency needs to put front-end filters on their collection of data, and stop recording conversations of Americans, unless a warrant exists. Violations of the 4th, 5th and 6th amendments all of course occur when Americans themselves are monitored for no good reason.

Let's look at some of Donald Trump's comments about this.

The real scandal here is that classified information is illegally given out by "intelligence" like candy. Very un-American!
— Donald J. Trump (@realDonaldTrump) February 15, 2017

Thank you to Eli Lake of The Bloomberg View – "The NSA & FBI...should not interfere in our politics...and is" Very serious situation for USA."
— Donald J. Trump (@realDonaldTrump) February 15, 2017

Information is being illegally given to the failing @nytimes & @washingtonpost by the intelligence community (NSA and FBI?). Just like Russia.
— Donald J. Trump (@realDonaldTrump) February 15, 2017

I've said it before – Trump knows everything and he is relentless. He is in process of taking these people down. This is a year when everything is being disclosed.

THE FALSE NARRATIVES OF OBAMA

Also during the Obama administration we had Edward Snowden. Snowden's story is just not believable. Snowden's story is that he is a high school dropout, and he also dropped out of a community college. He wound up making $122,000 at the Agency. He worked for the CIA and the NSA, starting out as a security guard for the NSA. Afterwards, he was promoted to the CIA under diplomatic cover in Switzerland.

But wait – it gets better. He became a private contractor for the NSA at a military base in Japan. Finally he was promoted to Regional SIGINT Operations in Hawaii, working under corporate cover. In 2013 he is granted medical leave from the NSA. He goes to Hong Kong and begins a series of leaks to London newspapers with the assistance of a documentary filmmaker, Laura Poitras.

Finally the Russians offer him asylum. What is happening here? Is he a red herring? Did someone use him to act against the NSA? Some loyalists to the former administration did not care to pursue radical Islamic terrorism. The NSA is in the forefront of this fight. The NSA is our last line of defense in the war against radical Islam.

The ultimate aim of the globalists is to destroy our intelligence agencies, and the military. And the highest art of psyops, psychological warfare, is to disinform the public. It's not accomplished by spreading lies, but by a one-sided and very artful selection of half-truths.

The American people are frankly tired about the lies that "Russian hackers have influenced the election results." The truth about this provocation is coming out now. On December 8th, US media have quoted Georgia's Secretary of State Brian Kemp as saying that he had tracked the origin of a hacker attack on his voter registration database and it was traced to an IP address of the Department of Homeland Security.

In a letter to Department of Homeland Security Jeh Johnson, Georgia's Secretary of State Brian Kemp said the state had discovered an unsuccessful attempt to breach the firewall of state computer systems. That attempt was linked to an IP address associated with DHS, he said.

The Secretary of State's full letter can be viewed here:

https://www.scribd.com/document/333663630/Letter-to-Jeh-Johnson-DHS#download&from_embed

Part of the letter states:

"At no time has my office agreed to or permitted DHS to conduct penetration testing or security scans of our network," wrote Mr. Kemp, a Republican. "Moreover, your department has not contacted my office since this unsuccessful incident to alert us of any security event that would require testing or scanning of our network."

The attempted intrusion was detected by a third-party security firm working for the state of Georgia.

According to a letter written by Kemp to DHS Secretary Jeh Johnson, the attempted intrusion occurred one week after the election on November 15, 2016 at 8:43 AM and came from an IP address associated with DHS (216.81.81.80).

This incident was followed by an attempt to simply continue to blame, without any evidence, unnamed "Russian hackers" for the election results. A press release by the Russian government has stated, "We can only add that if Washington takes new hostile steps, it will receive an answer." The full formal response from Russia can be viewed here:

http://www.businessinsider.com/russia-response-us-sanctions-2016-12

This is an ominous declaration – the globalists have placed us on the verge of World War III with Russia.

It appears obvious that Obama was determined to start World War III in his last days in office. Events are transpiring even now that threaten the Republic and all of our lives. Will the final spark be a direct confrontation in Syria, the Ukraine or Cyberspace? Obama accused the Russians of having influenced the election and, since the New World Order lost, this makes them desperate.

In terms of alleged Russian hacking, Trump states, "There is no evidence" and I agree with him. Perhaps the psyops department of one of the Intel agencies will attempt to generate false flag information. Nevertheless, both sanctions and threat of covert action were initiated by Obama in his last desperate days in office.

Various establishment (New World Order globalist) Senators agree (of course) with Obama's crazed strategy, which is leading us to the brink of war. This is just a bald assertion by the New World Order group; there is no act or event to justify these actions. The Russians know this was made up as well. As Senator Rand Paul has stated, Senator McCain would put us on a permanent war footing if he could. He cannot.

ILLUMINATI PLANS FOR AMERICA

My Pet Goat was the story being read in a children's classroom in Florida by George W. Bush during the first 9/11 event. Louis Lefebvre created the short film *I, Pet Goat 2* and describes it as based on a dream he had—a prophetic dream. He spent years putting it into production, paying for it himself. It has had several million views on YouTube.

This dream portends destructive plans by the New World Order. It's worth analyzing as it instructs us about the deep background of the matrix.

Now Louis Lefebvre says, "This film is designed to allow people to give it whatever meaning they want to project onto it." He adds, "Symbolism is just a language."

In the first part of the film, Bush's hat is pointing toward a shark, while he looks to the East Coast of the U.S., which is then eerily illumined.

We are taken through a doorway in the opening scene, where a wooden handle is used to open the door to a goat locked in a wooden box. It is right behind a barbed wire fence.

The scene of course is alluding to a FEMA camp. The goat has a barcode on its head; this is the 666 RFID chip. This is what has been planned, but President Trump has brought it to a halt.

The "Beast" in the Book of Revelation is referenced by the image of a dragon and this is the power behind such institutions as the globalist banks and also the governments. In the spiritual dimension, an army of evil is assigned to protect those who currently hold the power positions in this movement.

In the images, the glazed-over look that we see the goat go into represents how most humans have been dumbed down by the corrupt systems. They've lost the ability to think critically and cannot recognize what is happening right before their eyes.

Did you notice that after reading the words that the teacher was pointing to with her pointer, the children were asked to take out their books from under their chairs? This essentially was a bowing ritual as they all reached down to get their books.

Order must be formed out of chaos is *ORDO AB CHAO*, which is a motto of the Illuminati (i.e. senior Freemasonry).

The hidden hand of the actual Elite or the puppetmaster moves the strings of the public politicians to make them act just the right way at the right time. We know there's no gold to back the currency system in the U.S. It's a pure fiat money system which can collapse upon any catalyst.

The mainstream media uses psyops—distractions to move the public away from the truth. The real problems and the real players are masked. In this video, you see the players (Bush and Obama), who are behind the hidden hand of the small group of families who run the monetary system of the world—the Committee of 300—which includes the Rothschilds, the Rockefellers and the Council on Foreign Relations (CFR). These are the ones who pull all of the strings.

Notice the Masonic designs on the floor—the Masonic checkerboard floor signifies that this entire charade has a ritual component to it. Bush morphs into a smiling Obama and the dunce cap becomes a graduation cap, signifying that the world is now waking up by the time Obama is in power. A good percentage of the population, close to 50%, is aware of what is going on. We are more educated, largely because of the free expression of speech in books and videos on the World Wide Web.

This YouTube analysis of *I, Pet Goat 2* is very complete and takes you through the main points of the video:

https://www.youtube.com/watch?v=Tiz2WLB2Z0o

THE SHADOW GOVERNMENT AND JFK

In memoriam to my stepfather, who took the JFK autopsy photos, I'd like to introduce the JFK conspiracy. It has elements not unlike the current status of the New World Order—a variety of legends, covers, psyops and disinformation exist. The comparisons are striking and can educate us. It's a lesson text in critical thinking.

The single most important piece of evidence of conspiracy was that trained U.S. Army Intelligence units were told their assistance was not needed in Dallas during the JFK trip. William McKinney, a former member of the 112th Military Intelligence Group at 4th Army Headquarters, Fort Sam Houston, Texas, went public and stated that both Col. Maximillian Reich and his deputy, Lt. Col. Joel Cabaza, protested "violently" when they were told to "stand down" rather than report with their units for duty in support of the Secret Service in Dallas. All the Secret Service had to do was nod and then these units, who had been trained at the Army's top Intelligence school at Camp Holabird, Maryland, would have performed their normal function of protection for President Kennedy in Dallas.

The motorcycle escort was reduced to only four men, who were instructed to ride behind the rear wheels of the limousine. Two agents stayed with the plane at Love Field. Open windows along the route remained opened. Manhole covers were not welded shut. The crowd simply spilled over into the street.

Then the vehicles were in the wrong sequence. The Lincoln was first—it should have been in the middle. Any security expert would have detected this level of breach of protocol.

The route was changed only days before the arrival and included a turn of more than 90 degrees—a violation of Secret Service protocol. After bullets were fired, the driver pulled the limo to the left and actually slowed down. At the hospital, a bucket of water and a sponge were used to wash and clean up the crime scene.

The limousine was returned to Ford and on November 25th it was stripped to metal and rebuilt. The windshield had a through-and-through bullet hole in it, noticed by officials at Parkland. It was replaced.

David W. Mantik, M.D., Ph.D., has proven JFK was hit four times—in the throat from in front, in the back from behind and twice in the head both from in front and behind. Connally was hit at least once from the side—as he was turning to the left—and at least one shot had missed. That's six shots—not the official three. That proves conspiracy.

The purpose of the disinformation operation in the death of JFK was not really to convince the public of the official account. It just created enough uncertainty to make nothing knowable. A hastily but clumsily written disinformation report, authored by the Warren Commission, superseded any real investigations.

JFK, while in office, had transitioned from a traditional cold warrior into a statesman for peace, which threatened the status quo. He was about to take action on the oil depletion allowance, threatening major Texas oil interests. He had refused to invade Cuba, thus going against the advice of the Joint Chiefs. He was engaging a Vietnam withdrawal, which is a war many profiteers wanted. He also spoke against empowering Israel with nuclear capability.

Kennedy was going to reform or abolish the FED and, perhaps most important of all, he was going to "shatter the CIA into a thousand pieces." This statement that he released may have been the fatal one.

Finally, when New Orleans District Attorney Garrison tried Clay Shaw, the judge ruled out key evidence which indeed did tie him to his true identity and the crime itself. It was commonly known in New Orleans that Clay Shaw used the alias Clay Bertrand. A massive disinformation campaign was mounted by the Justice Department to quash Garrison and 17 witnesses mysteriously died before they could testify.

Clay Shaw, under the name of Clay or Clem Bertrand, was overheard planning the assassination of President Kennedy with David Ferrie and Lee Harvey Oswald, during the middle of September, 1963, in New Orleans. Garrison produced a witness who told a three-judge criminal district court panel on March 14, 1967, that he heard Lee Harvey Oswald, Clay Shaw and David Ferrie plotting to assassinate President John F. Kennedy.

Perry Raymond Russo, 25, an insurance salesman and from Baton Rouge, testified he was in Ferrie's apartment in New Orleans in September, 1963, and overheard a discussion of how to kill Kennedy and make a getaway. Russo said the plot involved "triangulation of crossfire," diversionary shooting and the sacrificing of one man as a patsy to allow the others to escape.

Undoubtedly, they reported to higher authorities, but Shaw's involvement with the CIA speaks for itself. It was revealed years later that he was a contract agent for the CIA. There's no doubt who the higher authorities were. President Kennedy was not the first target of the Permindex Assassination Bureau—a French Intelligence dossier on the company singled it out as funneling $200,000 to the OAS in the attempted assassination of de Gaulle a year earlier.

Oliver Stone was very close in his movie, but he didn't name names. For the amazing details of how far down the rabbit hole this money laundering went and who were the principals behind it, just read The Permindex Dossier, a Lyndon LaRouche study. It reveals the secrets of the JFK mystery that have been withheld from the public for decades. It reveals everything.

DONALD TRUMP'S LIGHTNING WAR AGAINST THE NEW WORLD ORDER

There are elements trying to overthrow the US via globalism, bringing in millions of illegal immigrants–putting them on welfare and then moving us to permanent war status to bankrupt the country. These people are called globalists and are known as the "New World Order." The politicians are of course bought and paid for.

Trump is beyond all of this. He has watched the global situation for 30 years. Trump has accomplished long, patient planning. He is a world builder. Trump was hidden in plain sight for years.

Trump camouflaged himself for years–he is a rare combination of skill and intelligence.

The enemy is squirming and scared. They don't know what to do. One major fake news channel, which shall remain unnamed, is losing money and failing. Their commentators are weak and stupid. The media says they have free speech, but we have free speech to counter them.

Private university studies indicate that California alone has added four million illegal voters to their rolls. Here's what Trump does–he is brilliant. He makes a statement and then with that statement, such as saying he won the popular vote, he baits the lamestream, mainstream media. Then he waits until a predetermined time to publish that which he already knows and then he calls them out for what they are, which is fake news. The major newspapers in New York and Washington are examples of fake news.

These people (mainstream news) are bush-league propagandists along the line of Germany in the 1940s. They are just as transparent. They know nothing at all. Their articles and opinions totally lack substance and rarely if ever have any factual basis. It's pure psyops (psychological operations)–and they're not very good at it.

Trump is the New World Order's worst nightmare. I'm certain he already has a plan in place to stop George Soros, who is funding the treasonous activities against the United States. He will be extradited to a neutral country and arrested by authorities.

Trump has recused himself from the Clinton Crime Family investigation. With Jeff Sessions as Attorney General, the noose will tighten there. The pay-for-play action was transparent and is provable beyond a reasonable doubt, according to Rudy Giuliani.

Trump's inauguration speech contained the strange words: "We stand at the birth of a new millennium, ready to unlock the mysteries of space." I believe this is a veiled reference to Nibiru. Donald Trump said what he could. Of course, I disclose the full story in my book Planet X – The 2017 Arrival. This is a major conspiracy and cover up. Trump knows. He signaled us with that statement, saying just enough for those listening.

The New World Order and the Establishment spent tens of millions of dollars to take him down and could not. As long as Trump is in power, the One World Government plan has come to a screeching halt.

MASONIC POWERS

Masonic powers and other occult factions within the governments of Britain, America and Europe hold a great many secrets. You are about to uncover the most guarded secrets.

Two royal families in Great Britain believe themselves to be descendants of Israel, but they are not. These are the current House of Windsor (Queen Elizabeth II, Charles and William) and the Scottish House of Stewart/Spencer (the late Princess Diana). The arranged marriage of Diana and Charles was of ancient design. Revelation 2:9 exposes this truth; it states a very cryptic message: "I know the blasphemy of them which say they are Jews, and are not, but are the Synagogue of Satan."

In 1969, at his royal investiture, the Red Dragon (again directly from the Book of Revelation) was presented on green and white banners. Queen Elizabeth II spoke directly from the Book of Revelation to Charles, "This Dragon now gives you your power, your throne and your authority." Charles responded, "I am now your liege-man and worthy of your earthly worship." A liege-man means Lord or Master. This is all right from the Bible, in Revelation 13.

"There are dark forces in this country of which we know not of."
Queen Elizabeth II to Paul Burrel (a former servant of the British Royal Household) – October 1997

It's very sporting of her to give us that heads up.

Some individual in the future will have the intent to establish a one-world government, monetary system and a one world religion. This is what the New World Order is all about. But not as long as Donald J. Trump is President.

THE MANCHURIAN CANDIDATE

Americans with sense—Republican and Conservative American citizens—have watched with horror the results of the Obama administration. 70,000 factories have closed since NAFTA. Obamacare was a disaster. Planned Parenthood is still funded. The borders are not secure and there is $10 trillion in new debt. Need I go on?

Donald Trump has a new set of policies to change all of this. I agree with him. But they will cause utter chaos among the establishment. Mexico will be up in arms about the cost of the wall. I support it 1,000%. But then look at China—it's about time we got tough with them. But the trade deals are going to be dismantled and they will react emotionally and not logically. Trump as President will shake the system—he is a mover and a shaker.

Look at the historical record in the Bible. God uses unusual people: Nebuchadnezzar enslaved Israel for 70 years and then Cyrus allowed the construction of a Jewish temple. Pharaoh enslaved Egypt for 400 years. Titus, in 70 AD, burned Israel to the ground. Hitler was quite demonically energized, but the result of World War II was the safe housing of the Jewish people in the new state of Israel. God works in mysterious ways.

You know, I had an inspiration the other day: Of the 25 or so Democratic and Republican candidates, I noticed only Trump made this promise about relocating the embassy to Jerusalem and recognizing it as the capital. Moving the US embassy to Jerusalem and recognizing it as Israel's capital would signify that Trump will comply with US law as expressed in the Jerusalem Embassy Act of 1995. God promised in Genesis to Abraham a blessing on those who bless Israel. After Trump's commitment, I noticed no one could catch up to him – no one could stand in his way. When he set his mind to this commitment, he had the help of Almighty God.

OBAMA ALMOST PROVOKED THE RUSSIANS

A door to Pandora's Box was almost opened by Obama and Clinton. They had us on the verge of war with Russia. If it had remained open, what the Russians could have done might have eliminated 90% of American civilians within one year — leaving only 10% of our citizens to forage among the ruins. This belief is backed up by no less than a Congressional commission. A 2004 report by *The Presidential EMP Commission* was convened to examine the risks of an electromagnetic pulse weapon (EMP) exploding over the continental U.S.

An EMP blast knocks out the power grid, with devastation following: a lack of food, water supplies and power for warmth. If Vladimir Putin did not have a cool head like President Donald J. Trump in office, he might have implemented the ultimate solution to destroy the New World Order. Putin in fact believes he has nuclear superiority—both defensively and offensively. He can also protect 50% of his population with shelters in Moscow and built into the mountains.

Our sub captains are gridlocked — without orders from Washington they cannot do anything. An unexpected EMP attack would likely neutralize lines of communication so that nuclear launch codes cannot reach the submarine fleet.

Peter Pry wrote a book: *The Long Sunday*.

In this book, he states that just like the early morning hours of Sunday, December 7, 1941, we are not on alert. Pry has testified in fact before Congress, though I don't believe a lot of them got the message. He said America is NOT ready to go to war. Our guard is down. This is why President Trump is back to building the military.

Quoting from Pry's book some bullet points that explain the situation succinctly:

- U.S. conventional and nuclear forces have become "hollow" from long underinvestment in their modernization and basic maintenance.

- The U.S. Army has shrunk to its lowest level of active duty soldiers since before World War II.

- The U.S. Navy, according to former Defense Secretary Leon Panetta, has the "smallest number of ships since 1915."

- The U.S. Air Force, according to Defense Secretary Panetta, "is the smallest Air Force in its history."

- U.S. strategic nuclear weapons are decades old and obsolete compared to brand new missiles and new generation nuclear weapons being deployed by Russia and China.

- The U.S. has ceded to Russia and China a virtual monopoly in tactical nuclear weapons, retaining only some 180 aged gravity bombs stored in European NATO, while Russia has an estimated 3,000 - 8,000 tactical nuclear weapons for battlefield and theater use.

- North Korea makes more nuclear weapons every year than the United States, which prohibits itself from making more nuclear weapons or replacing old weapons with new designs.

- European NATO has become so militarily "hollow" that RAND and the U.S. Defense Department estimate Russia could roll over NATO's frontline states in Poland and the Baltics in 60 hours. "President Vladimir Putin himself has said that Russian troops could be in five NATO capitals in two days," according to former Defense Department official Keith Payne.

A singular EMP attack over the heartland of the U.S. is relatively simple from a logistical standpoint. You don't need a super-accurate guidance system.

You don't need the logistic problems with an ICBM. It is far easier to create and launch an EMP attack than any other type of attack and the consequences are devastating.

It explodes 30 kilometers above the ground, so there is no debris to disclose who launched it. Radars, satellites and their downlinks are all destroyed. The attacker can remain largely anonymous. Forensic analysis cannot identify the perpetrator—there are no fingerprints.

An EMP attack is the ultimate cyber-weapon. In fact, some believe for purposes of strategy it might be combined with an attack upon half a dozen main coastal cities.

While we challenge Russia with words, Putin knows he can destroy all electronics with an EMP. Russia, China and North Korea all have EMP weaponry. North Korea has a satellite with EMP weaponry. We are a society built on electronics. We will not survive without the power grid. We must prepare ourselves individually and as a nation. Don't be concerned – Trump knows all about this.

DECEPTION BY THE ALPHABET AGENCIES

Intelligence agencies are obviously attempting to compromise the integrity of the Internet and any major topic discussed on it. If you see comments on book reviews or YouTube videos that are highly emotionally-charged, off-the-wall, totally illogical or indicating huge levels of bias, they do not come from normal individuals.

The Joint Threat Research Intelligence Group is a unit of the Government Communications Headquarters representing British intelligence. The existence of JTRIG was revealed as part of the global surveillance disclosures by NBC News in documents leaked by former National Security Agency contractor Edward Snowden.

Their "dirty trick" tactics are partly derived from their document entitled "The Art of Deception: Training for Online Covert Operations." After reading this document, I would say that if I owned a website, I would *not allow comments* since you are destined to attract, if the subject is at all controversial, these groups and their strategies. Just deny them the option. As Shakespeare said, "Less is better."

It enhances the appearance of most websites not to have these crazy comments by people who obviously either have mental issues or more than likely are organized trolls. Personally, I just don't see the need for publishing comments constantly—or at all. A website stands on its own authority. It doesn't need to cater to marginal individuals who add absolutely nothing.

These people, it has been discovered, monitor not only websites but YouTube and Blogger; these are the same people who during the last generation used "honey traps" and overreaching lies to discredit those who were properly going about their business. It's an attempt to control and manipulate. They have the objective of destroying the reputation of the target (site or individual). Why give them permission?

GCHQ describes the purpose of the JTRIG in very clear terms: "... using online techniques to make something happen ... including information ops (influence or disruption)."

These people are pushing the limits. These surveillance agencies have vested themselves with the authority to destroy a person's reputation. Unless you tow their political line, you are a target. I thought we had a First Amendment. You don't require a license to write or publish.

I have a best-selling book (Planet X – The 2017 Arrival) and I consistently get 80% great reviews and about 20% negative reviews. I happened to be watching a well-known psychologist on TV and he said something interesting. He said close to 20% of people have mental problems. No wonder – that explains it. I wish they'd stay on their medicine and not attempt to write book reviews.

These covert agents and pseudo-independent advocates infiltrate online groups and websites. These GCHQ documents now prove that a major Western government (thanks to Wikileaks) are disseminating deception online. These are "false flag operations." These powers are exercised in secret, with no oversight. George Orwell in his book said we would eventually reach this stage.

THE CONTRACTORS FOR THE ELITE

You have to understand how the Intelligence community operates. When Eisenhower warned of a "vast military-industrial complex," he wasn't kidding. Of course, he provided no detail, but he was fully aware of it. Case in point: he authorized Area 51, but then received absolutely no information from it. He finally had to send two representatives out there and threaten the base with an Army invasion if they didn't disclose what they were doing. This has now come out as common knowledge.

What happened is that they immediately "compartmentalized" the operation on a need-to-know basis, restricting total knowledge to only a few people. Nothing was produced in writing, of course. This is how the Intel community, which is a generous name for them, operates. They have a $6.5 trillion black-ops budget. That's the latest number for missing money from the Pentagon.

How do they use it? Well, first and foremost, Deep Underground Bunkers for the elite. Secondly, they use it for special operations — often the CIA and the DIA (Defense Intelligence Agency) operate in tandem. The CIA sets up the operation and the DIA covert or black-ops people run it. These are not people you'll see on TV or in uniforms. They wear suits, blend in and when operating do not even use their real names.

They operate, many of them, out of sub-level offices in otherwise innocuous-appearing office buildings around Virginia and Washington. They have no accountability. They have access to special units of contractors for whatever they need.

THE GOALS OF THE NEW WORLD ORDER

The globalist, New World Order agenda has been soundly defeated and they know it. They have been totally exposed. The fact that six of their corporations control the media is known to all. They are dishonest and seeking a hidden agenda.

The goals of the New World Order started in 1776. One day in May of 1776 Johann Adam Weishaupt founded the "Illuminati" in the Electorate of Bavaria. He adopted the name of Brother Spartacus within the order.

The New World Order has moved behind the scenes ever since. It had its hand in everything from the French Revolution to the establishment of the secret and private so-called Federal Reserve.

In August of 1910 Senator Nelson Aldrich sent his private railroad car to the New Jersey Railway Station to rendezvous with six other men who were instructed to come under conditions of great secrecy. They were told not to be seen together - two of the men adopted code names. Absolute secrecy was essential. The train traveled for two days and nights, and ended at Brunswick, Georgia. They then proceeded to Jekyll Island.

For years they denied this meeting took place until after the Federal Reserve was established. Of course we know the Federal Reserve is about as federal as Federal Express. It is a private consortium of international banks. Aldrich was the grandfather of Nelson Rockefeller. The Rockefellers are proxies of the Rothschilds in America. The Federal Reserve is an unaudited, unaccountable organization of private international banking interests. This organization, often referred to as "The Creature From Jekyll Island," was established at this meeting. Enter Donald Trump – I have indications he is going to require this shadow entity to be audited.

Fast forwarding – in August, 1990, President George H.W. Bush condemned the invasion of Kuwait by Iraq. He solemnly declared, "This invasion threatens the New World Order." He was a believer in the New World Order system, which incorporates belief in a single ruler (of the world), a single currency and a single religion, all enforced by the RFID chip system. Don't these people themselves realize that they also would be subject to the whims of this madman whom they want so desperately in power?

The New World Order has destabilized relations with Russia. The U.S. launched a ground-based missile defense system in Romania, right on the Russian border. Putin is concerned it could turn nuclear and offensive at a moment's notice, totally upsetting the "geopolitical balance of power" that has existed for decades and which has also kept any one superpower from achieving a nuclear or offensive advantage.

Russian President Vladimir Putin warns he'll retaliate against NATO missiles.

Ukraine was a Playbook CIA coup d'état of the New World Order.

The New World Order has brought us very close to the brink of nuclear destruction with World War III. Then came along Donald J. Trump. Against the controlled media and psychological operations of the New World Order, his movement succeeded in proportions unlike anything we have ever seen. His instincts have proven amazing and he has taken on the New World Order in his speeches and his policy decisions and Cabinet appointments.

WAR IN SYRIA

To review the past to learn from it, I just watched a Reuters interview with Donald Trump in which he said if Hillary were elected we will be in a world war with Syria and Russia in a matter of weeks. She doesn't know what she is doing.

In addition to the absolute insanity of her idea of a no-fly zone in Syria, which would be an immediate declaration of war with Russia, there is also the possibility that Erdogan, the strongman in Turkey, will continue his policy of placing troops right up to and at the *Red Line* in Turkey. He is supposedly protecting his "clients" in Syria. In any case, once he moves those troops over the *Red Line*, Putin will have no alternative but to strike. With only 20,000 troops in Syria, Russia will be forced to use strategic nuclear weapons. An attack on Turkey is an attack on NATO and thus you have World War III as well in this scenario.

In the proxy war to date this year, America has authorized the destruction of a headquarters building housing top Russian generals, all killed in the attack. Russia has bombed a CIA/Mossad HQ in Syria, killing all of the people involved. These events often precede a declaration of war.

Here's a must-see video (produced by Alex Jones) which is the best summary to date:

https://www.youtube.com/watch?v=xuH5Utoiazg

American Intel has released data on *Satan 2* which is a term they've coined for a Russian MIRV with 14 40-megaton warheads. It travels at Mach 6 and cannot be stopped. Just one of these can take out an area the size of France. Unbelievable ... the times we are in.

To use a Marine motto, *Godspeed and smooth sailing to us all.*

BEHOLD, A PALE HORSE

The election was about critical issues – Liberty versus the New World Order agenda. It's about honesty and integrity versus old school shadow politics.

This book describes avenues of alternative investments which will be impervious to the financial collapse we are shortly facing. These investments and the economic truth behind them are detailed in this one-of-a-kind briefing manual.

Above and beyond the economy, what happened in November will trigger world events that will uniquely affect this generation with an impact never before seen. Vladimir Putin of Russia understands this. He calls Donald Trump "a bright person" and says he will invigorate US-Russian relationships. He says no such thing about Clinton.

Putin, like Trump, knows the hidden agenda. He knows the delusions of the globalists. He knows their desire for a one-world government, currency and religion. And he knows the fallacies of their beliefs. A one-world, new order was the dream of the ancient Greek philosophers, who were just as wrong as the ones who subscribe to the Illuminati philosophy of the New World Order today. A one-world government will have an all-powerful leader and by history we know those men have evil intent. The world is designed to have several hundred nations with independent and primarily democratic leaders. But absolute power always means absolute corruption.

Putin of Russia is the former head of the KGB. He thinks like an Intelligence Analyst, which he is. The failed Obama directives which Clinton would have enacted, would have continued, for example, to not only initialize but expand the dreaded anti-missile system in Romania. Putin calls this a tragic error. He realizes it is not only defensive but can be converted on a moment's notice to an offensive threat right at Russia's borders and destabilize the delicate balance of geopolitical security. The missiles can be switched from nonnuclear to nuclear without the government of Romania evening knowing about it, since it's a US-NATO operation. If this policy is enacted to its fullest, then we are at a DEFCON ONE Threat Level for nuclear war with Russia. Putin has as much said this. Those missiles, right at his border, can fire inland right now up to 500 kilometers. This is another critical difference between the candidate of Liberty, Donald Trump, and the delusional New World Order adherents. Russia is our primary political-military concern – and we must have someone in office who can deal with them.

Bill Clinton was a student of Carroll Quigley, a New World Order proponent under the guise of intellectualism. Hillary Clinton has publicly stated that it's wonderful that the Council on Foreign Relations is just down the street from the State Department because she doesn't have that far to go for advice. This is a tacit admission of complicity. The doomed mission at Benghazi is but a pale forewarning of following globalist agendas.

In my opinion the Bilderberg annual meetings violate the Logan Act. These New World Order globalists meet annually at the top resorts in the world, usually a hundred to a hundred and fifty of them, and they discuss the micro-management of U.S. and globalist agendas. Henry Kissinger is always among them – that gives you a major clue right there to anyone listening.

CONTROLLING U.S. PRESIDENTS

Let's flash back briefly. The globalists have proven adept at even controlling U.S. presidents. The Royal Institute of International Affairs' plan to oust Nixon was called Watergate. He was instructed not to bomb Hanoi, nor to invade Cambodia. Students of the conspiracy believe it was Alexander Haig who played the role of confusing and brainwashing Nixon, while Henry Kissinger then took control of the White House.

Haig was most likely the code-named "Deep Throat" who provided the guidance and direction that allowed Woodward and Bernstein to uncover the machinations of Nixon's inner circle. This was a major coup. The Watergate incident was a not-so-veiled warning against future presidents to not cross the line. The Committee of 300 thinks they have everyone within their reach.

Going back a little further – in 1964, after the contrived Gulf of Tonkin incident, U.S. aircraft carriers had been stationed offshore and a "war" was started. Jet planes would take off from the carriers to perform their bombing missions. Unused ordinance would be dropped in safe drop zones before landing back on the carriers.

Observers noted that many of the smaller explosions occurring almost daily in the South China Sea waters and thought they were part of the war. This was Operation Linebacker One — Standard Oil began its ten-year oil survey of Vietnam's seabed. No one was the wiser. The U.S. taxpayers paid for it.

When Standard Oil had enough data, the war ended. Vietnam proceeded to divide their offshore coastal areas into oil lots and allowed foreign companies to bid on them. Royal Dutch Shell, Russia, Germany and Australia all won bids. Strangely, none of them discovered oil. However, Standard Oil's lots for which they had bid all proved to have vast oil reserves. Research pays off, I suppose.

Obviously, they use covers and legends, as in those examples of their modus operandi. *Through the Looking-Glass* is the mentality we have to adopt to understand the forces at work. Seeing how they have operated in the past is part of our required study.

THE COMMITTEE OF 300

You really have to understand the Committee of 300, the governing body of the New World Order, to understand why and how the cover up takes place.

The Committee of 300 works through the Royal Institute of International Affairs in London, the Aspen Institute and the Club of Rome – all possess various executive arms. I was told this by an MI6 intelligence officer. These arms also include the Council of Foreign Relations, from which the US Secretary of State has drawn until now their strategies almost entirely; therefore, following the socialist party line. If you control the Secretary of State, you control all foreign policy.

The Constitution is immutable but the so-called progressives or socialists interpret it in a flexible manner. Thus, the President can declare war without going through a five-step Constitutionally-required process. All he needs is a 'vote' from the United Nations.

Woodrow Wilson was a major leftist under whom the Federal Reserve was established. Before the Reserve and the graduated income tax, we had a $5 billion dollar surplus through trade tariffs. Both the Reserve and the income tax saw to it that the extreme opposite would occur.

However, in leaving office, Wilson spoke a veiled statement acknowledging the presence of the Committee of 300:

"Some of the biggest men in the United States, in the field of commerce and manufacturing, are afraid of somebody, are afraid of something. They know that there is a power somewhere, so organized, so subtle, so watchful, so interlocked, so pervasive, that they had better not speak above their breath when they speak in condemnation of it."

The "power" Wilson was talking about is the Committee of 300 and Wilson knew he did not dare to mention it by name.

When Mikhail Gorbachev announced in the United States he was forming a foundation, CNN was filming it and Gorbachev plainly stated, "We have the approval of the Committee of 300." That transcript, later requested, was never acknowledged. But he had been at the very top of the elite's power structure and he knew it.

The Committee of 300 includes many royal families of European heritage as well as the Rothschilds and their US proxies, the Rockefellers. It includes some very dangerous people.

The Committee of 300 is interested in a New World Order and in accomplishing this objective they have a new spirituality, called the New Age Movement. They desire a single ruler of the world with a global currency. The only major country to actively resist the New World Order concept is Russia, which the group is actively and strategically plotting against. However, Russia is a world superpower and Vladimir Putin is a very smart man. The Committee of 300 is quite aware that their coalition will not include Russia.

Their paid disinformation specialists, some of them at alphabet agencies, are very cunning. But they are not smart – they are only deceptive.

One of the few presidents to actively go against their agenda was John F. Kennedy. My stepfather was a critical player in this drama. He was part of the autopsy team at Bethesda Naval Hospital. He told me that within 48 hours of the autopsy the entire medical team had been threatened and muzzled. He never spoke of it again. He was paid off – with a pension. So were others.

THE NEWS BEHIND THE NEWS

What the world calls history is theater. We need to study the "news behind the news." Most young people today are so plugged into their electronic devices and fed so much disinformation and misinformation by the mass media, they have ceased to effectively even function. This is what the powers that be count on.

As far as true history goes, universities now for the most part no longer pursue the old concepts of chivalry, critical thinking and truth. Instead, they're devoted to social engineering and "getting everyone on the same page."

History is propaganda about the past. Most historians don't tell the truth or they would be fired. History is replete with cover-ups and conspiracies.

You've probably heard of the United Kingdom's Government Communications Headquarters, also known as GCHQ. If you haven't, be assured they've heard of you. If you used the World Wide Web from 2007 forward, they have probably logged your entries into their database. *Karma Police*, a harmless-sounding code name, is the name for their data-mining operation, the largest in the world, designed to track "every visible user on the Internet."

According to GCHQ, by 2009 the program had stored over 1.1 trillion "events"—Web browsing sessions—in its "Black Hole" database. By 2010, the system was gathering 30 billion records per day of Internet traffic metadata. According to another GCHQ document, that volume grew to 50 billion per day by 2012. Who knows where it is today?

THE SECRETS OF WORLD WAR II

Between 1935 and 1951, the Soviets knew all of Britain's secrets through the Cambridge Five. This team operated in MI-5, MI-6 and the Foreign Office. Baron Rothschild was the Fifth Man, protected until his death.

Was Hitler raised to power by an unseen hand?

Standard Oil supplied the Nazis with fuel. It supplied a rare lead additive without which the Luftwaffe could not fly.

Situated on a slight rise – formerly known as Affenstein Hill – in Frankfurt Germany's desirable WestEnd district is a remarkable building. The I.G. Farben Building. General Eisenhower gave specific instructions at the time of the Allied bombing of Frankfurt to avoid damage to the Farben Building. It later became CIA Headquarters in Germany.

Adolf Hitler was totally dependent on the industrialists who put him in power.

In the end war criminals either went to work for the CIA or fled to South America.

What we term history is mostly propaganda, a cover-up. FDR said nothing in politics happens by chance.

FACTS

In 1952, Dwight D. Eisenhower said: "We have been unable to unearth one bit of tangible evidence of Hitler's death. Many people believed that Hitler escaped from Berlin."

Judge Michael Musmanno (of the Nuremberg Trials) said in 1946: "Hitler's body was never found." In 1948 he said: "We have no evidence that he died in his bunker or anywhere."

In 1945 Red Army General Zhukov said: "We have found no corpse that can be Hitler's. I am absolutely, positively sure Hitler escaped from Berlin."

Nikita Khrushchev said: "Yes...sure...Stalin did not believe Hitler committed suicide. I am certain he did not shoot himself in his bunker."

Stalin, in May of 1945, told Harry Hopkins, U.S. envoy: "It is my opinion that Hitler is not dead. He is alive and hiding somewhere. I wish your government will understand and accept this..."

Newly declassified FBI documents reveal that the Bureau was aware of a submarine that made its way up the coast of Argentina, and dropped off high-ranking Nazi Party officials including Hitler. The FBI was tipped by one informant that Hitler was living in the foothills of the Andes.

In 1945 a Los Angeles informant asked for asylum in exchange for information. What he told agents stunned them. He was one of four men who had actually met the German submarine. Hitler and Eva Braun were among the occupants.

Argentina at that time was a center of Nazi wealth. Billions of dollars which had been stolen from the countries, art galleries, people and banking institutions of the countries the Germans had conquered had been funneled to purchase massive ranches, businesses and banking infrastructure in Argentina, all in preparation for relocation of Adolf Hitler himself. The government in Argentina was an active and willing participant, according to informants. This exact document can be viewed at the FBI's vault at:

https://vault.fbi.gov/adolf-hitler/adolf-hitler-part-01-of-04/view

This link is actual online FBI source data – a description by various informants of the landing of Hitler in Argentina as just described. Over 200 more pages of detailed information follow this report at this link. This has only recently been declassified.

The cover story was a suicide. It was actually a homicide. And the supposed skull of the victim, Hitler, was taken to Russia to the State Archive. There it resided until it was tested several years ago by a University in Connecticut for DNA. The conclusion: it was the skull of a young female, somewhere between 20 and 40 years of age.

In terms of dental records, a normal form of identification, this never occurred since Hitler had authorized his personal dentist to destroy all records. Hitler had employed four doubles during his reign, and he knew well their purpose and their end. No step was overlooked. The destruction of his personal papers and files is a historical fact.

In 1943, as the first year of Hitler's escape plan became operational, Admiral Doenitz was known to have said publicly: "The German U-boat fleet is proud to have made an earthly paradise, an impregnable fortress for the Fuhrer, somewhere in the world."

To get to Argentina required getting Hitler and Eva to a safe port. General Franco, the military dictator of Spain, was a close friend of Hitler and had thus achieved neutrality for Spain during the conflict. A large German infrastructure had been in place in Spain. Spain provided access to deep water ports for German U-boats.

The only tactical measure required was to move Hitler and Eva from their Bunker to the airport, several miles away, and then fly them to Spain. This was accomplished through a secret door within the bunker, which led to a German tunnel that underscored the entire city. The exit panel could be reached by a hidden doorway in Hitler's bunker. The tunnel was constructed by Albert Speer. It was known to the German military as the underground railway network. Today the same tunnel is used as a subway and guess where it leads – right to the entrance to the Berlin airport.

It is a known fact that a variety of flights out of this airport occurred the week before Berlin fell. On April 22, 1945 ten separate flights carrying top Nazi officers left the Tempelhof Airport. These were the connected Nazis.

Hitler's personal pilot, Hans Baur, told Russians who were interrogating him that: "Adolf Hitler, Eva Braun and General Hermann Fegelein escaped aboard a Ju 52 Aircraft."

Lt. Colonel Walter Horten in 1946 said that "I never doubted it (the Escape). Borman planned it well, and Admiral Doenitz knew exactly what to do..."

The Allies were vastly more interested in capturing General Dr. Hans Kammler, who was conceivably worth "billions in terms of intelligence and scientific information," and of course recruiting Dr. von Braun. These now-declassified documents reveal the journey to Spain and the trip to Argentina – the true story of the Escape of Hitler.

Russia has finally completed DNA testing on the remains of "Hitler and Eva Braun" and determined that neither one is actually Hitler or Braun. This is the smoking gun – proof of Hitler's escape.

If Hitler can escape and the majority of the American people be totally unawares, and the officials (the FBI and others) never properly investigate, what does that tell you about the **coup d'état** against Donald J. Trump? This is the reason the book was written – to expose the darkness and give you an Intelligence Briefing about how to survive a coming global economic reset. Donald Trump said: "I inherited a mess." That's his clue to a coming global economic reset. My name is David Meade and I wrote this book to provide a way out. We are facing a global economic reset. The stock market is a mirage. This set of circumstances provides a never-before-imagined buying opportunity.

THE NEW WORLD ORDER COLLAPSE

Time is of the essence. Let's review the Clintons for a moment. The Clintons, among others, have left Donald Trump "a mess" in his own words. That's his code for being on the precipice of a global economic collapse. Her husband Bill laid the groundwork for the Dot.com bubble, and the ruinous hyperinflation of real estate values. NAFTA was another disaster, destroying millions of American jobs. The economy, already on the precipice, is on the verge of collapsing over the cliff. Massive stock market withdrawals by certain institutions will occur at a future predetermined date.

In 1999 Bill Clinton repealed Glass-Steagall. The next 7-8 years was the Roaring Twenties all over again. Banks created fraudulent loans – sham transactions including the so-call "Collateralized Debt Obligations" – they actually sold this stuff to the American public and investors. Guess what? In 2008 the house of cards collapsed.

Clinton is a "New World Order" proponent, and as such she has done major damage to Middle East stability and the safety of Israel. She bows to the demands of the Council on Foreign Relations.

Instead of deregulating and drawing on Alaska's oil, which would make America energy-independent, she relies on failed old-school policies to conquer and control Middle East oil. Obama has released billions to Iran, which they are using against us – they are the #1 terror state in the world. The New World Order would keep people everywhere from deciding their own destinies by means of one created crisis after another and then "managing" such crises.

Obamacare has devastated the medical community. The USA has the highest debt level of any nation in the world. We need to go into survivalist mode from a standpoint of major investment diversification, and right now.

Most importantly, this book leads you to the last chapter "The End Game." This is a detail description of where New World Order policies are purposely and secretly leading America. It is a revelation every American needs to know. The Clintons have been referred to as agents of the "establishment" or the "shadow government" by various commentators. Their hidden agenda, which I know Donald Trump is very aware of, is revealed for the first time here. The book takes you step-by-step from the outer reaches to the inner core of what is about to befall America.

As a pragmatist and an investor, I would say time is very, very short and you need to start preparing today. This is going to be more of a climb up Mt. Everest than a predictable Swiss train ride. You need a guidebook – this is it.

After 2010, most bears were looking for either a long sideways bear market à la 1966-1982, or a hyperinflationary run to infinity. My premise is that the most likely profile is a stock market crash of historic proportions.

This bear market is of a Super-cycle degree, the biggest since 1720-1784. It should therefore include a decline deeper that the 89% decline of 1929-1932. A decline of 91.5% or more would carry it below 2,000.

Whether it carries it to a low of 3,000 or 1,000 is immaterial. Tremendous profits are made on the swing, during the bottom and afterwards. The rest of this book is all about the protection of capital.

Have the tremors begun? Watch this ten-minute video. You have to think like a contrarian. As Donald Trump said, quoting Thomas Jefferson, and I'm paraphrasing – don't buy into or believe anything you read in the newspapers (and that includes the talking heads on the money channels).

https://youtu.be/uHitSnQBiTE

Gold, Gold stocks, and my favorite play of Silver are all covered in this edition. There are also 3x ETF funds that can take advantage of Bear market behavior.

This book will show you the cycles, analyze the inevitable outcome and give you the information you need to profit from the coming economic collapse. Get ready for the most amazing buying opportunity of your lifetime. Gold strategies, silver strategies, gold stock strategies and much more are covered in this one-of-a-kind manual. One of the mottos of the Navy SEAL training programs is: "You must plan as if everything that can go wrong will, because one misstep, one malfunction in planning or execution could cost the life of a brother." This is your financial life – if you're still with me, and this book isn't for everyone, then read on. This book, like all documents I produce, is a mission-specific briefing, in a class of its own. It will enable you to live through what is about to happen, and not even bat an eye.

"There's no shortcut to any destination worth going." UNKNOWN

This book covers:
- The Causes of the Coming Global Economic Crash
- World Gold Shares
- How to Develop a Gold and Silver Portfolio
- Silver Investing
- Alternative Investing
- Creative Non-Paradigm Planning and Thinking
- The Real New World Order End Game

I'm the author of 10 books. I've written Intelligence Briefings for some of the largest corporations in the world, and know how to analyze and disseminate intelligence, a rare talent. I'm a strategic planner unlike anyone you've ever met. Enjoy this book!

Let's continue our journey.

David Meade

NEW WORLD ORDER MACHINATIONS FOR A GREAT DEPRESSION

The Great Depression is going to happen, but you can profit from it. In this book Investigative Journalist David Meade explains how. A chilling look at the facts, graphs and cycles behind America's next economic collapse.

There is a pattern of economic crashes occurring every seven years dating back to the Great Depression. The Great Depression suffered its worst year in 1931, then later we have the Arab Oil Embargo, the S&L crisis, Black Monday, the 1994 Bond Massacre, the 2001 NASDAQ crash, and the 2008-2009 Financial Collapse. Each occurred at the very end of a 7-year economic cycle. We are now overdue. Regardless of the timing, though, it will happen and this book will prepare you and tell you why it will occur.

We are on the verge of the greatest depression in history, and with it the most opportunity to profit. The premise of this book is that the Dow Jones will continue to increase its phantom expansion until it reaches a totally unsustainable level, and then will collapse to the 15,000 level, from which it will collapse even further without a recovery. When this happens silver will become the most undervalued asset in the world and will be three digits in value, over $100 an ounce and soon thereafter many multiples higher.

There is a plan to destroy the US Dollar and not to pay back the 100 Trillion in unfunded liabilities. The elite would prefer to simply transfer their personal holdings to Euros and gold. Their plan is to divest American assets, sell the dollar, renege on all debts and start with a brand new currency. That plan is revealed here. The End Game is spelled out.

A favorite quote from a friend of mine who studied this book...

"Never before has this measure of Intel Briefing occurred in one book. It has priceless actionable Intelligence. This is the SEAL TEAM 6 briefing on the New World Order and True Economics."

Jim Rickards, a CIA consultant and Investment Banker, states in his best-selling book *The Death of Money* that the United States will enter into an Economic Depression of over 10 years duration soon. It is inevitable, he says. It will begin with a 70-80% stock market decline. One of the flashpoints is that Russia and China have stopped buying and started liquidating treasuries, and they are no longer trading in petrodollars. This is major and hardly reported by the news media. Therefore much of America is clueless. A wide variety of flashpoints will create the crisis. A $100 Trillion dollar liquidation is right before us.

I recommend one primary investment medium above all others. That is silver, in the form of U.S. Mint-produced American Silver Eagle coins.

Silver: From $20/oz. to over $500. It's going to happen for three main reasons, and it will happen soon. First, for decades there was a 10 Billion ounce government surplus of silver. <u>It is now entirely depleted.</u>

Second, the price of silver has been manipulated for years. It's called the "London Silver Fix" by some analysts. Several international banks in London teleconference on a daily basis, every day at noon London time, and benchmark the price of silver. Bids are exchanged and the price is fixed at an equilibrium point. <u>This practice officially ended August 14, 2014.</u>

Third, when the economic collapse occurs, let's look at the amount of funds held in US Banks. It's 18 trillion. 1% of that is $180 billion. Since most silver is consumed for industrial purposes, the above-ground supply has been variously estimated at 700 million ounces (new mine supply) to one billion ounces. Let's use the new mine supply. Divide that into the 180 billion of new money seeking silver and you have a price of $257. per ounce. But that excludes non-U.S. purchases and industrial use. These forces will be buying silver, and that differential should take the price up to the $500 range. If 2% of the public wakes up, then you have a $1,000 price.

Source of silver calculations:

Hommel, J. (2011, January 13). Silver: From $30/oz to over $500 by 2020 - SilverSeek.com. Retrieved from http://news.silverseek.com/GoldIsMoney/1294902060.php

American Silver Eagle Quick Facts and Brief History

The Silver Eagle is 1 Troy Ounce of 99.9% pure silver bullion.

The design is "Walking Liberty" - featuring Lady Liberty gliding confidently toward the sun.

American Eagle silver bullion coins were first released by the U.S. Mint in November 1986 under the Liberty Coin Act, passed the year before. Minted each year since, the American Silver Eagle coin was first created in the San Francisco Mint, then the Philadelphia Mint and now West Point. The U.S. Mint also produces proof sets each year.

American Eagle silver bullion coins are one of the easiest and affordable ways to invest in precious metals. U.S. law allows these silver bullion coins to be included in an IRA retirement account, presenting additional tax benefits as well. Investors can buy American Eagle silver bullion coins individually or in a Box of 500 (bulk pricing applies for most dealers).

What is the maximum price of silver I project? It's really simple and based on supply and demand. As Bix Wier states (Road to Roota website and book), you have:

1 Billion Ounces of above-ground silver available for investment purposes

5 billion Ounces of above-ground gold available for investment purposes

The scarcity factor is 5/1 in favor of silver. With $1200 gold (rounded - presently), that equates to a price when monetary or investment demand enters the equation of 5 times $1200 or $6,000 per ounce of silver. It's very realistic in my opinion.

RUSSIA ABANDONS THE DOLLAR

The Russians have made an unprecedented move against the petrodollar. Russia owns Gazprom, the largest natural gas producer in the world. They have signed agreements with their customers to move payments from dollars to euros. The Russian government owns the majority stake, so this was done with Putin's approval in a plan to destroy the dollar.

The mainstream media hasn't issued a word about this. But it is huge news. Gazprom is a massive operation, one of the largest corporations in the world — it constitutes 8% of the Russian GDP, and it is responsible for 18% of the natural gas reserves of this planet. And it represents a sudden, striking departure from the use of the dollar as a reserve currency.

Why did the Russians do this? It happened shortly after Obama slapped some sanctions on Russia due to their invasion of the Ukraine. The Russians, however, have not forgotten.

Source:

Snyder, Michael. "Russia Is Doing It - Russia Is Actually Abandoning The Dollar." The Economic Collapse. Last modified June 10, 2014. http://theeconomiccollapseblog.com/archives/russia-is-doing-it-russia-is-actually-abandoning-the-dollar.

IS THE LEVIATHAN GAS FIELD THE LARGEST NATURAL GAS FIELD IN THE WORLD?

The Leviathan Gas Field is located off the coast of Israel, and may be the world's largest, with more natural gas reserves than the combined fields of Iraq and Saudi Arabia. The potential reserve size is estimated at ***16 trillion cubic feet!***

Russia is interested in being a major player in the Leviathan natural gas field, according to an Israeli foreign affairs analyst, Ehud Yaari. Until now Prime Minister Netanyahu had ruled out a Gazprom/Russian deal, but now with the high level of military presence of Russia in Syria, Netanyahu may reconsider.

He said Mr. Putin had told Mr. Netanyahu: "We will make sure there will be no provocation against the gas fields by Hezbollah or Hamas. Nobody messes with us."

Disputes over the development of this vast field of natural resources could lead to major war in the region. If this happens, the price of oil could skyrocket to over $200 an ounce and this could be the driver of a major worldwide economic collapse. It's one of many trigger points that could actuate the next Depression.

IS GLOBAL ECONOMIC COLLAPSE UNAVOIDABLE?

"The Bank for International Settlements (BIS), describes the current situation at the world´s financial markets as worse than before the crash of Lehman Brothers. In its quarterly report, the BIS described the situation as critical and directly mentioned the possible end of the deluge of paper money. Experts imply the risk of a sudden, overnight financial crash.

The situation now is worse than prior to the Lehman Brothers crash, said White to the British newspaper The Telegraph. White points out that:

All the previous imbalances are still there. Total public and private debt levels are 30pc higher as a share of GDP in the advanced economies than they were then, and we have added a whole new problem with bubbles in emerging markets that are ending in a boom-bust cycle".

Source:

Lehmann, C. (2013, September 25). Global Economic Crash has become Unavoidable | nsnbc international. Retrieved from http://nsnbc.me/2013/09/25/global-economic-crash-become-unavoidable/

Among other peculiarities in the news, the U.S. recently denied Germany an audit of the gold reserves. And a shipment of gold from Ft. Knox to China was tested at the Chinese border. They chose 4 400-ounce bars and drilled into them. They found that the bars were only gold-plated, and there was a tungsten core.

I hate to tell you this – it may come as news – but you cannot trust the government.

On top of all of this, the World Bank's Chief Economist, Kaushik Basu, recently stated a "wall of debt is coming at us." That's very sportsmanlike to let us know.

DERIVATIVES PANIC IN GLOBAL MARKETS

The derivatives market is 10 times the size of the annual GDP of the world! The Bank of International Settlements in 2012 reported its size at $638 trillion. Some authors claim it is much larger, on the size of $1.2 billion. Let's compare this to the size of the GDP of the world - $65 trillion. The value of the US stock market is $23 trillion (Economist Magazine).

Derivatives pose a threat to world economic stability because once losses appear, it may be impossible for financial institutions to cover them. This could take down the world financial system as we know it. These products are almost totally unregulated. Zero accountability accompanies them.

When President Bill Clinton signed the Gramm-Leach-Billey Act in 1999, this removed the Glass-Steagall law which had acted as a buffer and prevented commercial and investment banking to exist together. This led to the current status of where we are now. Great decision, Bill! Afterwards derivatives exploded from $30 trillion to the astronomical level of today. Let's look at some of the banks:

- **Deutsche Bank** – $55.6 trillion in derivatives exposure as of April 2013 backed by only $575 billion in assets. So their derivatives exposure is 96 times larger than their assets.

- **JP Morgan** – $72 trillion in derivatives exposure compared to only $2.3 trillion in total assets. Their derivatives exposure is 31 times larger than their assets.

- **Goldman Sachs** – $41 trillion in derivatives exposure compared to only $938 billion in total assets. Their derivatives exposure is 43 times larger than their assets.

- **Citigroup Inc** – $57 trillion in derivatives exposure compared to only $1.9 trillion in total assets. Their derivatives exposure is 30 times larger than their assets.

- **Bank of America** – $44 trillion in derivatives exposure compared to only $2.2 trillion in total assets. Their derivatives exposure is 20 times larger than their assets.

- **Wells Fargo** – $44 trillion in derivatives exposure compared to only $1.3 trillion in total assets. Their derivatives exposure is 33 times larger than their assets.

(Source: FDIC and SNL Financial for US institutions, Zerohedge.com for Deutsche Bank)

There is no way these institutions could cover the potential losses.

When the United States stock market crashed in October 1929 there was no such thing as derivatives and the national debt was only 16% of the annual GDP, a fraction of today's statistics. These factors combined together could make the coming economic collapse far worse than the 1929 stock market crash.

Several widely-known billionaires have recently left Israel, and recently divested most of their stock holdings. Could they know something we don't know?

Source:

http://Z3news.com

http://z3news.com/w/derivative-panic-coming-global-markets/

THE MAINSTAY OF PRECIOUS METALS

"I believe that banking institutions are more dangerous to our liberties than standing armies. If the American people ever allow private banks to control the issue of their currency, first by inflation, then by deflation, the banks and corporations that will grow up around the banks will deprive the people of all property until their children wake up homeless on the continent their fathers conquered. The issuing power should be taken from the banks and restored to the people, to whom it properly belongs."

Thomas Jefferson
3rd president of US (1743 - 1826)

In 2013 the German Bundesbank demanded the repatriation of a large part of its gold reserves which were held abroad. By the year 2020, Germany wants half of its total physical gold reserves back in the Frankfurt vault. This includes a demand on the Federal Reserve for 300 tons. The Federal Reserve has not permitted an audit of its gold holdings as requested by the German government. The dollar is no longer a safe haven currency. This German demand for the gold, if immediately granted, would have in effect been a run on the Federal Reserve. This cannot be allowed to happen by insiders.

To date there have been LIBOR (London Interbank interest rate) scandals, an energy price scandal and a credit default swap scandal. Do you really believe that the price of gold and silver are not artificially held down way, way below their true market values? How long can this continue? How can increasing demand by central banks and investors lead to a price which doesn't escalate dramatically?

This whole scenario is nonsensical. It's an attempt to keep the global bond market stable, and this plan is failing. Whistleblowers tell us that manipulation is taking place. JP Morgan shorted 3.3 billion ounces of silver some years ago. These large investment houses are constantly sued for fraud, and in other countries for corruption. Do you really believe their forecasts?

The Federal Reserve is clearly out of its depth. It's the "greatest hedge fund in history." Once gold breaks $2,000., the average investor will realize the Federal Reserve's control is broken, and world traders could see $10,000. - $15,000. gold and $500 silver.

Gold is the only true value of wealth. The elite buy it. There are in excess of 55 paper gold contracts to every 1 physical gold contract. That's why it is important to buy gold - physical gold and silver. Even the producers around the world that spend up to the maximum – say $1,000 an ounce – to bring gold out of the ground will shortly see the price increase by a manifold amount, but their cost to produce will remain virtually the same. Thus the leverage of the gold stock investment. It could reach 10 or 15 to 1, or even more.

Paper investments are just that – paper. Retirement funds are often held in paper. You'll need a significant amount of your personal assets invested in precious metals to survive what is coming. Exchange Traded Funds (ETFs) are good to hedge and move counter to the market with leverage. But you need core holdings in real assets.

Fiat paper currency has gone down in country after country. Gerald Celente, in his *Trends Journal,* states that gold is being manipulated by the U.S. central bank and also by the European central bank. They rig the game buying bonds and treasuries. Celente says he buys precious metals, and he is "not a speculator." They are for his retirement. He also says about the central governments: "they are never going to solve this problem." It is unsolvable. The only solution is a major devaluation or crash, or a combination. Germany years ago experienced a hyperinflationary crash which left its currency worthless. It was transported in wheelbarrows.

U.S. inflationary policy has accomplished much the same, but we're not there yet. Still, $1 in 1913 compared to the current status of the dollar is an interesting comparison. It requires close to $24.00 to buy what that one dollar bought then. On the other hand, gold has increased from about $20. an ounce in 1913, to close to 60 times that rate in recent years. Which is the better investment?

The Federal Reserve is so leveraged it is technically bankrupt, as we'll discuss in a future chapter. The U.S. is borrowing trillions annually to "balance" its budget. Read about the currency crash in Zimbabwe and you'll get an education of what may happen right here. Zimbabwe faced 231 million percent hyperinflation and crashed its own currency.

The dollar is no longer the petrodollar king. All oil transactions used to be carried out with the dollar. China now trades its own currency, the Yuan, for oil purchases. Russia is backing them. The former respect for the dollar as an international reserve currency simply no longer exists. China may stop buying U.S. debt entirely. China, Russia, Brazil, and South Africa have the largest gold and silver reserves in the world. **Anglo American plc** is a multinational mining company headquartered in London, United Kingdom. It is the world's largest producer of platinum, with around 40% of world output, and a major producer of diamonds, copper, nickel, iron ore and metallurgical and thermal coal. They are one company everyone should consider investing in.

Banks in the U.S. trade in derivatives, and that market is approaching $1000 Trillion dollars. Back at the last economic crisis it was only $500 Trillion. It just takes a small correction to crash this market. The interest on U.S. debt is now unsustainable. All the while there is betting going on through the derivatives market.

Banks are in a peculiar position. They can borrow from the Fed at 1.25%. Why do they have any interest at all in backing small businesses with the attendant risk?

The Fed can make one remark and cause the market to go to a standstill position and crash. When the Fed said it was going to "taper off" qualitative easing, or buy less open market positions, back in June of 2013, this one remark caused the market to drop. The 7-day repo benchmark (interbank) went from 3.3% to 8.26% in one day! The following day it was 12.33% in China, and one major Chinese bank ran out of liquidity. An interest rate climb can crash the currency and the economy. It's that simple. Banks can close just like they have in the past.

The derivatives market may be used to crash the economy. If interest rates increase and stay up, $400 Trillion or more in derivative value will be lost. The Bank of International Settlements (BIS) has stated that the current scenario is worse than the status quo before Lehman went bankrupt. Global credit excesses are much, much worse. 2007 and 2008 will not be repeated, accorded to BIS. It will be much worse.

The list is too long to mention, but other governments during monetary crises have liquidated excess savings from their citizens through their own banking systems. Check out Cyprus, among others. There's a Mexican billionaire named Hugo Salinas Price. He says that the rise in interest rates may be what is used to precipitate the next crash, and we'll have in my opinion only days or hours of notice. The derivatives market will fail.

Here is an excerpt from a recent interview with Mr. Price:

> "Last year the Bundesbank reported that it would repatriate all of its gold reserves from Paris and part of them supposedly located in New York, in the 2013 – 2020 period. Nevertheless, last year they repatriated merely 37 tons and only five tons from the NY Fed. In your opinion, what would be the reason for this delay?
>
> The reason is crystal clear: the US does not have the gold is says it has. The US was the custodian of a gold cookie-jar, and the US government simply ate up the cookies. They have no gold left." (1)

Gold remains a true value among all other failing options. If you have assets when no one else does, you can buy what you need and want for pennies on the dollar. Bernard Baruch did. You can, also. Remember, those who stay in dollars and paper will lose the vast majority of their assets. If you have liquidity when no one else does, this is the key.

(1) Source:

http://www.silverdoctors.com/billionaire-hugo-salinas-price-gold-is-the-feds-enemy/

SEVEN EXPERTS WHO AGREE WITH ME

"Don't let me screw up." - *The mantra of all SEAL Teams.*

From around the world...

The Jerome Levy Forecast: "Clearly the direction of most of the recent global economic news suggests movement toward a downturn."

John Ing: "The 2008 collapse was just a dress rehearsal compared to what the world is going to face this time around. This time we have governments which are even more highly leveraged than the private sector was."

Bill Fleckenstein: "They are trying to make the stock market go up and drag the economy along with it. It's not going to work. There's going to be a big accident. When people realize that it's all a charade, the dollar will tank, the stock market will tank, and hopefully bond markets will tank. Gold will rally in that period of time because it's done what it's done because people have assumed complete infallibility on the part of the central bankers."

Paul C. Roberts: "At any time the Western house of cards could collapse. It (the financial system) is a house of cards. **There are no economic fundamentals that support stock prices — the Dow Jones.** There are no economic fundamentals that support the strong dollar..."

Phoenix Capital: "Just about everything will be hit as well. Most of the 'recovery' of the last five years has been fueled by cheap borrowed Dollars. Now that the US Dollar has broken out of a multi-year range, you're going to see more and more 'risk assets' (read: projects or investments fueled by borrowed Dollars) blow up. Oil is just the beginning, not a standalone story.

If things really pick up steam, there's over $9 TRILLION worth of potential explosions waiting in the wings. Imagine if the entire economies of both

Germany and Japan exploded and you've got a decent idea of the size of the potential impact on the financial system."

Gerald Celente: "What are they going to do? They can't raise interest rates. We saw what happened in the beginning of December when the equity markets started to unravel. So it will be a loss of confidence in the con game and the con game is soon coming to an end. That is when you are going to see panic on Wall Street and around the world."

Rob Kirby: "What this breakdown in the crude oil price is going to do is spawn another financial crisis. It will be tied to the junk debt that has been issued to finance the shale oil plays in North America. It is reported to be in the area of half a trillion dollars worth of junk debt that is held largely on the books of large financial institutions in the western world. When these bonds start to fail, they will jeopardize the future of these financial institutions. I do believe that will be the signal for the Fed to come riding to the rescue with QE4. I also think QE4 is likely going to be accompanied by bank bail-ins because we all know all western world countries have adopted bail-in legislation in their most recent budgets. The financial elites are engineering the excuse for their next round of money printing . . . and they will be confiscating money out of savings accounts and pension accounts. That's what I think is coming in the very near future."

THE PLAN TO OVERTHROW THE U.S. ECONOMY BY THE NWO

"Cheer up, comrades. Things will get worse." – RUSSIAN SAYING

In 2008, the Federal Reserve bailed out the U.S. institutions that were headed into default. The International Monetary Fund (IMF) is minimally leveraged and could bail out the Federal Reserve in another crisis. The IMF is populated for the most part by the non-elected, including Communists, dictators and New World Order advocates, including representatives of the Rothschild family. Could this be who takes over the world monetary system and could this become the central bank of the world? Their currency is called Special Drawing Rights. It's the currency of the New World Order.

U.S. macroeconomic policy and current status are probably the most important topic one can study. A variety of scholars, government specialists and think tanks concentrate on this field of study. One of them is Jim Rickards, a veteran (three decades) with Wall Street's largest investment firms. He helped build the technology of the NASDAQ. He has testified before Congressional committees. He is the CIA's Financial Threat and Asymmetric Warfare Advisor. He and other academics have noted a series of highly dangerous economic flashpoints that will affect the U.S. markets momentarily. Just as Dr. Nouriel Roubini testified before Congress just before the 2008 economic meltdown, and very few listened, these individuals have accumulated large amounts of macroeconomic data which should be of concern to every one of us. This section will investigate the current status of the U.S. economy.

Over the last six years, over $3.1 trillion has flooded our economy. U.S. total debt now stands at close to $20 trillion. In addition, there are $126 trillion in unfunded liabilities. These are Medicaid, Medicare, social security, student loans and Freddie Mac and Fannie Mae liabilities.

The U.S. is experiencing a vast decrease in the velocity of money. In 1970, for every dollar of debt created there was $2.41 of economic growth. In 1980 this velocity was at $3.50 in growth. Today that number has exponentially decreased to $1.45 in growth for each dollar of debt.

Inflation rates constitute another critical economic metric. Combined with high unemployment rates these continuing inflation rates lead to social instability. A 29% decrease in value of one's dollar holdings over the period January of 2004 to October of 2014 is illustrated by a government chart. To obtain the percentage, we simply deduct the beginning balance (188.5) from the ending balance of value (243.34), and divide the significant difference by the beginning value to obtain the percentage decline.

Gross Domestic Product (GDP) is the market value of goods and services produced by the United States during a time frame. It measures wealth and indicates an expected return on invested capital. It is an excellent gauge of the health of an economy. The Federal Reserve uses these statistics to fine tune its view of society's needs.

The history of the GDP tells us a lot if we analyze it. In 2003 the growth rate was 2.8%. That year unemployment held steady at 6%. The Federal Reserve lowered its interest rate to 1%. That was the year the Iraq War began.

In 2004 we saw a growth rate of 3.8%. The Federal Reserve began raising rates.

In 2005 the growth rate was 3.3%. Hurricane Katrina caused $250 Billion in damage to the U.S. infrastructure.

In 2006 a 2.7% growth rate exists. The Federal funds rate was raised to 6.75%.

In 2007 a 1.8% growth rate existed. The Dow reached a new high of 14,164. Inflation was at 4.1%. The Federal Reserve dropped the rate three times, finally to 4.25%. The London Interbank (LIBOR) rate rose to 5.6%.

In 2008, not surprisingly, the growth rate was a negative .3%. The stock market crash led to a global liquidity crisis. $350 Billion was spent just on bank bailouts. The Federal Reserve lowered the rate 7 times, and finally to 0%.

In 2009 a negative 2.8% growth rate exists. The Dow dropped to 6,594. An additional stimulus of $400 million stopped the downward spiral.

In 2010 the growth rate was 2.5%. This was the year of the BP oil spill, and tax cuts were continued.

In 2011 the growth rate is 1.6%. The ten-year Treasury yield hit a 200-year low point in its index.

In 2012 the growth rate is 2.3%, and in 2013 2.2%.

A major decline in the Baltic Dry Index portended the 2008 crash.

The Baltic Dry Index is a measure of the cost of shipping dry goods such as the cost of shipping iron ore from South Africa to Tokyo. In 2008, the Index triggered a warning signal for the meltdown that was imminent. It is a totally independent measure and not subject to market manipulation by anyone. Brokers in London set the Index based on the daily fluctuations in the cost of moving wheat, oil and commodities around the world. Falling, it indicates a slackening of demand on a global scale. When the Index fell by 66 percent in 2008, it provided an independent benchmark for investors who were watching. Just Google it and study the chart as of today. Enough said.

The Federal Reserve responded to the 2007 – 2008 financial collapse. It rapidly reduced the targeted federal funds rate from 5 ¼% to zero. This represented an extraordinary ease in the U.S. monetary policy. The Federal Reserve provides short-term liquidity to banks and does so through its Term Auction Facility, Primary Dealer Credit and Term Securities Lending Departments. Bilateral currency swaps occurred with a variety of foreign banks. They eased dollar liquidity with the Central Banks.

In addition in responding to the economics of 2007-2008, the Federal Reserve expanded open market operations to the credit markets. They placed downward pressure on longer interest rates, and purchased agency-guaranteed mortgage-backed bonds to support recovery.

Economic data indicates that the vast majority of U.S. workers, including both white and blue-collar workers, endured a period of wage stagnation from 2003 to 2013. Wage growth has underperformed productivity growth.

Between 2007 and 2012 wages fell for the lowest 70 percentile of the wage distribution while at the same time productivity increased 7.7%, an anomaly and an indicator of a systemic problem with U.S. economic policy.

Wage growth in the earlier years of 2000 – 2012 was propelled by a momentum of the late 1990s, the Internet boom period. But between 2002 and 2012 a period of wage stagnation was observed. This amounts to a *lost decade* for most wage earners.

The Recession of 2008 offered evidence that global securitization was a false premise. Large banks were buying hundreds of thousands of packages of mortgages known as Collateralized Debt Obligations (CDOs). These were marketed to pensions and other accredited purchasers, who were incorrect in assuming they were buying AAA or investment quality debt. The sub-prime factor was not disclosed. The risk model was ignored.

In 2008 the major Investment Banks took on risks for which they had no capital base to allow. The leverage was astronomical. Looking back to the fall of Long Term Capital Management in 1998, the 2008 Recession was a duplicate of this event on a major scale. If a bank leverages 10:1, which is not unusual, and then it collapses, that causes a $2 Trillion credit contraction. The major Investment Banks were leveraging 30:1 and even higher, and off-balance sheet risks were at 100:1.

The Federal Reserve's current capital is estimated at $56.2 billion. That sounds very substantial, but in comparison to the total balance sheet, how significant is it? How much in the way of liabilities is that amount of capital supporting?

Senator Rand Paul stated in recent congressional testimony, made official as a Capitol transcript, that we learned this year that the Federal Reserve's balance sheet has reached to the level of over $4 trillion in liabilities. In perspective, this is larger than the entire economy of Germany (U.S. Capitol Transcript, 2014). The Federal Reserve had a leverage of 22 to 1 prior to 2008 ($22 in debt for every $1 in capital). The leverage today is 77 to 1.

Senator Rand Paul stated on the floor of the Senate that he has repeatedly called for transparency at the Federal Reserve. The Investigator General (who is responsible for auditing the Federal Reserve) in public testimony stated that she did not have jurisdiction to audit the Reserve Bank. There is no audit of the Reserve Bank (U.S. Capitol Transcript, 2014).

At a minimum, aren't American taxpayers entitled to know what is happening behind the curtain? The "Federal Reserve" is owned by a consortium of private international banks.

Dollars were historically backed by gold but they are now backed by promises. How long the international community, which is now buying that very commodity through its Central Banks, will allow the dollar to remain king and the petrodollar to rule in world markets is questionable. The gold window was closed by President Nixon in 1971, ending the value derived from the dollar by its tie to that metal and standard.

The Federal Reserve is leveraged 77 to 1, with about $55 billion in equity and $4 Trillion in obligations. This is higher leverage than was experienced by Lehman Brothers or Bear Stearns before they failed.

The Federal Reserve is insolvent on a mark-to-market basis. However, the Reserve carries its notes at cost and therefore avoids the technical definition of bankruptcy.

Was the panic of 2008 a harbinger of a far worse event that has not yet transpired? Nobel Prize winner Robert Schiller (Yale) has indicated that the recent 12% rise in housing prices is extremely rapid and probably indicates another bubble (U.S. Capitol Transcript, 2014).

China has downgraded U.S. debt, and some believe the debt level is only manageable with the Federal Reserve buying it. China has stated that our government borrowing has outpaced all realistic economic growth. What will happen if interest rates quadruple?

A bipartisan bill has been introduced, the Federal Reserve Transparency Act, known by its name as Audit the Fed. This would eliminate the restrictions on the General Accounting Office (GAO) audits of the Reserve Bank. This would also bring their activities under congressional oversight. Their current level of privacy and some say secrecy would have to become transparent.

One of the signs that are really fundamental, and really important, is the ratio of the value of the stock market to the Gross Domestic Product (GDP). Currently the ratio is 203%. In 2008 the number was 183%. In 2004 it was 110%. Just prior to the Great Depression it was 87%. In other words, the same metric is more than twice as high today as it was in 1929. This is compounded by the Gross Notional Value of Derivatives in the world today, over $700 trillion. This is a factor of more than ten times the global GDP.

The inherent macroeconomic risk is that foreign nations, including China and Russia, are engaged in a sell-off of treasuries. If no one buys them, then interest rates will go up. High interest rates will depress, very substantially, the U.S. stock market.

One other flashpoint which will have global macroeconomic repercussions is the replacement of the dollar as the world reserve currency. The International Monetary Fund actually has a public plan to replace the dollar, and it has been published as a report *The Dollar Reigns Supreme by Default* (Prasad, 2014). The plan is scheduled to take effect over a ten-year period but it may occur at any time. The report states that the status of the dollar is in peril due to the largely increased supply. If enough governments sell off enough dollars (that is, their Central Banks) and diversify into the Euro, perhaps the Swiss Franc and precious metals to diversify and protect their holdings and investments, then this would represent even another flashpoint for a macroeconomic crisis.

References

Benko, R. (2014, April 28). Is James Rickards Right About A Coming Monetary Apocalypse? Retrieved November 30, 2014, from http://www.forbes.com/sites/ralphbenko/2014/04/28/is-james-rickards-right-about-a-coming-monetary-apocalypse/

Hansen, S. (n.d.). Velocity of Money Slowdown Means No Inflation? - NOT. Retrieved November 30, 2014, from http://www.nasdaq.com/article/velocity-of-money-slowdown-means-no-inflation-not-cm405688

Prasad, E. (2014, March 1). The Dollar Reigns Supreme, by Default - Finance & Development, March 2014. Retrieved December 4, 2014, from http://www.imf.org/external/pubs/ft/fandd/2014/03/prasad.htm

Short, D. (2014, November 25). Visualizing GDP: A Look Inside the Q3 Second Estimate. Retrieved December 3, 2014, from http://www.advisorperspectives.com/dshort/updates/GDP-Components.php

U.S. Capitol Transcript. (n.d.). Emergency Unemployment Compensation Extension Act--Motion To Proceed-- Continued. Retrieved November 30, 2014, from http://capitolwords.org/date/2014/01/06/S15-2_emergency-unemployment-compensation-extension-act-/

U.S. Government. (n.d.). Databases, Tables & Calculators by Subject. Retrieved November 30, 2014, from http://data.bls.gov/pdq/SurveyOutputServlet?series_id=CUURA421SA0,CUUSA421SA0

UNDERSTANDING HISTORICAL COLLAPSES

A STUDY OF THE 2008 COLLAPSE

"There are no rules here – we're trying to accomplish something." - THOMAS EDISON

"I don't know about you, but I'm in it for the money."
– FROM THE MOVIE *THIRTEEN DAYS*, spoken by Kevin Costner to the actor portraying Robert Kennedy. You can take this comment as it was meant – a dark speech, dark comedic reference to the value of a government salary compared to those who actually control and run the high-level political establishment.

Dr. Tatyana Koryagina, a senior research fellow in the Institute of Macroeconomic Research in Moscow, stated in a Pravda interview that "the U.S. is engaged in a mortal economic game. The known history of civilization is merely the visible part of the iceberg. **"There is a shadow economy, shadow politics and a shadow history."** She went on to say, "It is possible to do anything to the U.S. Generally, the Western economy is at the boiling point now. Shadow financial activities (of $1000 trillion) are hanging over the planet. At any moment, they could fall on any stock exchange and cause panic and crash." She further stated, "The U.S. has been chosen as the object of financial attack because the financial center of the planet is located there." [1]

This is a very interesting statement from an individual who is known as a personal advisor to Vladimir Putin, the Russian Prime Minister. What do the Russians know - what is Vladimir Putin privy to? Why were institutions and individuals blindsided by the financial tsunami of 2008? They did not understand that liquidity can be an illusion. It is there when you don't need it but "gone with the wind" when you do.

Tatyana is telling us with some dark speech that the only thing we don't know about investing is the investment history we don't know. It's not necessarily confined to a matrix. We're in the very beginning stages, depending on who you listen to, of the worst financial crisis since the Great Depression. It's the 'shadow financial system' that has created the current crisis that we're in. The shadow financial system consists of non-bank financial institutions that, like banks, borrow short, and in liquid forms, and lend or invest long in less liquid assets. They are able to do this via the use of credit derivative instruments. The system includes SIVs (Structured Investment Vehicles), money market funds, monolines, investment banks, hedge funds and other non-bank financial institutions. These are subject to market risk, credit risk and particularly liquidity risk.

We have learned that Investment Banks (and active managers in general, such as hedge funds) cannot protect from bear markets. They themselves were unprotected. One exception (if you consider a 2-year history) were the **Paulson Credit Opportunities** and **Paulson Credit Opportunities** II hedge funds, which produced net **returns** of about 590% and 352% in **2007** and lesser returns of about 19% and 16% in **2008.** The Paulson Event Arbitrage Fund returned 100%, and the Paulson Merger Arbitrage fund returned 52.0% in 2007. The amount of money generated by Paulson and Co., both for themselves and their partners can only be described as ridiculous. These funds generated tens of billions of dollars in profit in 2007. If the fund operates with a traditional "2 and 20" (2% management fee, and 20% performance fee), that means that the fund likely generated at least 3-4 billion dollars in profits for the principals. Not a bad year. 2008 was more subdued. The primary leverage against the sub-prime market was effectively utilized in 2007 by these funds. I list these because they're an excellent example of principle – innovative think-tank type planning and execution. Once it was planned it was as good as done.

The opposite of this thinking is reflected in how the State of Florida happened to lose $ 61.4 Billion in state-administered funds in only a year and a half in 2008. The State Board of Administration protects $ 97.3 billion in pension money for retired state employees, and invests another $ 25.3 billion for school districts and state and local governments. A close friend of mine sat on the Board for ten years. Auditors warned them year after year about complex and high-risk investments but these warnings were ignored. The chief internal auditor who wrote one of the more recent reports stated "Risk is an inherent component of doing business. To appropriately manage risks, organizations should have mechanisms to identify, measure and monitor relevant key risks not only at the business or product level, but at the institutional level." The SBA took on real estate and private partnership investments, and added leverage to the equation. One investment, $ 5.4 Billion into an apartment complex in Manhattan, is now valued at 10% and Wall Street credit firms have downgraded bonds tied to the deal. They were also using complicated financial instruments called derivatives, which billionaire investor Warren Buffet once called "financial weapons of mass destruction."

In the 18-month period covered by the audit, the unit handled $ 1.1 trillion of transactions with limited oversight. One trader bet $ 1.4 billion on a single trade. The audit also revealed that the unit let an unauthorized trader, a trainee, deal a total of $ 30 billion in securities. In the audit period, 70% of the trades were done with only four brokers – Bank of America, Goldman Sachs, UBS and the now-defunct Lehman Brothers. While they delayed finalizing the audit, the 2006 State Legislature passed two bills allowing the SBA to use even riskier financial strategies, and the other made it more difficult for outsiders to scrutinize some SBA investments. In August 2007 they were finally required to attend risk training. Deloitte and Touché recently completed a $ 198,750. Investment Performance Risk Review and another firm has been hired for an approximately $ 182,500 contract (plus expenses). The SBA says it's a pittance and "money well spent."[2]

The auction-rate securities market, hundreds of billions, seized up in 2008. Indy Mac failed in 2008. Lehman left the country with a $ 168 Billion bankruptcy in 2008. The AIG entry into the credit default swap field required a government bailout in 2008. Hedge fund losses were huge, the worst in 15 years in 2008. The current crop of LBOs for the most part failed in 2008.

Let's look at Mortgage Backed Securities and CDOs at that point in time. The complex market for asset-backed securities took a major blow. A U.S. Federal Judge ruled to dismiss a claim by Deutsche Bank National Trust Company. The US subsidiary was seeking to take possession of fourteen homes from Cleveland residents living in them, in order to claim the assets. The Judge asked DB to show documents proving title. No mortgage was produced, needless to say. The net result is that hundreds of billions of dollars worth of CMOs in the past seven years are not securitized. One source places the number at $ 6.5 Trillion.

Global securitization was a phantom idea – when large banks bought tens of thousands of mortgages, bundled them into Jumbo securities and then had them rated prior to sale to pension funds or accredited investors, they believed they were selling (and the counterparties believed they were buying) AAA or at the least investment grade quality. They never realized the bundle contained a significant toxic factor rated "sub-prime." No one opened the risk models of those who bundled them.

In 2008 Investment Banks took on more risk than they had ability. Their baskets of risk were highly correlated. The leverage made no sense. When LTCM fell in 1998, this is exactly what happened. Banks as you know leverage 10:1 or greater. A $200 Billion loss in the financial system leads to a $2 Trillion contraction of credit. Lehman was at least 30:1 with just assets. Off-balance sheet risks were not considered which probably brought the leverage to over 100:1. Systemic damage has been done.

This was to date the worst financial crises this generation has ever faced. The housing sector was literally in free fall. Calculated Risk, a very credible web site, estimates that a 10% drop in prices will create 10.7 million households in default. A cumulative fall in home prices of 20% implies 13.7 million households with negative equity while a cumulative fall of 30% implies 20.3 million households with negative equity. What is the size of these losses for financial institutions and investors? If a 15% total price decline occurs, and a 50% average loss per mortgage, the losses for lenders and investors is in the $ 1 Trillion category. Assuming a 30% price decline you can double that.[3] The whole spectrum of financial and credit markets has been effected. Commercial real estate followed the trend of residential.

You have to consider geostrategic and long-term issues before allocating assets. This would include foreign policy, energy supply risks and bond and stock markets. You have to consider financial deleveraging on the currency market. You need to game out the scenarios of the IMF on this chess board, among many other players. Alternative investments holdings such as non-US denominated bonds (AAA rated in hard currencies), South African gold shares, direct holdings in strong currencies and diversifications into alternative investments are a must if you are to survive. Gold and silver are keys. Exchange Traded Funds (ETFs) are one holding mechanism.

A synopsis of reasons I believe this is correct is deductive logic from a Global Economic Analysis site: Roubini nailed three reasons for a severe recession but dismisses "L" because the U.S. acted faster than Japan.[3] I do not buy that argument for these reasons:

- U.S consumers are in much worse debt shape than Japan.

- There is global wage arbitrage now that did not exist to a huge degree in the mid to late 1990's. Even white collar jobs are increasingly at risk.

- The savings rate in the US is in far more need of repair than what Japan faced. This will be a huge drag on future spending and slow any recovery attempts.

- Japan faced a huge asset bubble (valuation) problem. The US faces both a valuation problem (what debt on the books is worth) and a rampant overcapacity issue as well.

- Japan had an internet boom to help smooth things out. There is no tech revolution on the horizon that will provide a huge source of jobs.[4]

93% of stock market newsletters lost major capital for the readers in 2008.

In fact, this has indirectly caused a boom in the class-action field. In 2008, the number of federal securities filings reached a six-year high, with 267 filings. That's a 37% increase from the previous year. Almost half were related to the credit crisis. Investors are claiming they have lost approximately $ 856 billion, according to the Stanford Law School Securities Class Action Clearinghouse. That's a 27% increase over 2007. Most of the actions are against firms in the financial industry. A director of Stanford Clearinghouse said he hasn't seen this much litigation against a single industry in over a decade. One-third of all major financial firms were named as defendants in these actions. Most of the cases allege securities fraud, or altering values. Underwriting practices were allegedly misrepresented. The firms that sold auction-rate securities, bonds with interest rates reset by bidding, were all hit with class-actions, as the market completely dried up last year.

Active mutual fund managers cannot protect anyone. Investors, both corporate and individual, took on risks they did not have the ability to handle. Many investors in the Madoff scheme were guilty themselves of concentrating virtually their entire portfolios in his hands.

***"The only difference between myself and a madman is that I am not mad"* - Salvador Dali.**

To re-balance your portfolio you've got to engage in sound leadership. You've got to devote a lot of due diligence to a Performance Review and game out scenarios just like the CIA does every day. I learned you cannot trust your future to Princeton economic professors – they work best only in ivory towers.

Bailouts, unless they are handled properly, can trigger a major devaluation of the dollar or lead the nation further into stagflation, then deflation and ultimately depression. The US debt position is approaching unsustainable levels.

Rense, a top alternative news source reference, in an article on economic protocols, reports:

> Therefore, if the planet can no longer generate any more liquidity to lend to the United States, one of three things have to happen: A) There has to be a sudden and dramatic reduction in federal spending. There are only two places that can come from. There would have to be an immediate cut in defense spending and entitlements. This is highly unlikely.
>
> The other option, B, is a dramatic increase in the rate of federal income taxation from the current nominal rate to 65%, which is what the Treasury Department estimated would be required post-2009 to provide the U.S. Treasury with sufficient revenues to continue to service debt.
>
> The third option, or C, becomes the declaration of a force majeure on credit service of U.S. Treasury debt by the United States Treasury, which is tantamount and would be accurately construed as de facto debt repudiation by the United States of America. That is the classic definition of a devaluation. What institutional and large corporate investors call 'fast market conditions' would occur. There would be the declaration of 'no more stop orders,' the declaration of 'fill at any price,' etc. in a desperate bid to maintain liquidity. [5]

Let's take a brief look at 2008:

- Housing – down 18% nationally and 30% plus in cities

- Emerging market funds – down 55%

- Bonds – Rates on 10 year Treasuries dropped 42%

- US Treasury yields – very low and for a time close to zero

- Bond values – down 6-24% on average depending on the funds and quality of bonds

- DJIA – down 33%

- S & P 500 – down 38%

- NASDAQ – down 40%

- Financial sector ETFs – down 55%

Protocols for environmental disasters are called 'scaling-circle scenarios.' 'Scaling circles' is a Department of Defense euphemism. It's also used in FEMA, OEM and other emergency management services. The risk has got to start someplace. It's going to start in one very small, specific area. Therefore what happens is that the immediate force containment is the greatest in the first circle, to try to contain the spread of the disaster and keep it within that circle. That's what you have to do.

You have to consider macroeconomics before you reposition your assets. You have to reposition assets. You have to close all major risks. Exit the majority of money funds and currency time deposits, step up gold and oil positions, and move into non-US government bonds in First World nations. Switzerland is a prime consideration, but there are first-class world banks with branches just a short flight from Florida. You have to modify your thinking as if you are on a special ops tour of duty. Otherwise the current toxic economic environment will continue to deplete non-repositioned assets.

[1] Nemets, Dr. Alexandra, Russian Expert Who Predicted Attacks Warns of New Ones, *http:archive.newsmax.com/archives/articles/2001/10/3/212706.shtml*

[2] Highlights and links to 39 reviews of the Florida State Board of Administration, *http://www.tampabay.com/specials/2009/graphics/SBA-audits/*

[3] Roubini, Dr. Nouriel, The Current U.S. Recession and the Risks of a Systemic Financial Crisis, Written Testimony for the House of Representatives, 2/26/08

[4] Shedlock, Mike, Case for an L-shaped Recession, *http://globaleconomicanalysis.blogspot.com/2008/04/case-for-l-shaped-recession.html*

[5] Martin, Al, Protocols For Economic Collapse In America, *http://www.rense.com/general80/protc.htm*

OIL, GEOPOLITICS AND WAR

"If you want to rule the world you need to control the oil. All the oil. Anywhere." MICHEL COLLON, MONOPOLY

Iran, Iraq, Kuwait and Saudi Arabia have more proven oil reserves under their soil than the rest of the world combined. Oil qualifies as the most vital commodity in existence today. The U.S. Department of Defense is the consumer of over 80% of the energy utilized by the federal government. In the early 1970s seven of the world's largest companies were in the oil business – Exxon, Mobil, Chevron, Texaco, Gulf, BP and Shell.

The U.S. has always had a keen interest in the Middle East. In 1953 the CIA organized a coup to install a U.S. ally, the Shah, to power. Israel plays a vital role in serving U.S. interests in the Middle East. Saudi Arabia was initially financed by a joint venture of SOCAL (Standard Oil of California) and Texaco, who won drilling rights in 1936 to large fields in that country. Saudi Arabia has 25 percent of the world's reserves, and the largest oil production facilities available in the world today. The House of Saud is the royal family of the Kingdom of Saudi Arabia. The modern nation of Saudi Arabia was established in 1932. Stability in the Middle East is now maintained by the presence of Israel together with Saudi Arabia. These two countries are steadfast friends of the United States and serve to contain radical groups that currently exist in that region or at least that's the theory.

OPEC (Organization of Petroleum Exporting Countries) was founded in 1960 by five key nations and later expanded by other nations of that region joining. Countries who are members of OPEC have negotiated quotas of oil production expected of them. 50% of the world's oil that is available for export is represented by OPEC. Saudi Arabia is the main player. OPEC has the ability to leverage and de-leverage production as required.

Some individuals have questioned whether the real purpose of the US invasion of Iraq was to obtain a source of cheap oil that allows the US to undermine OPEC, and other competitors as Russia. U.S. oil giants are interested in Iraq since it has reserves in excess of an estimated 112 billion barrels, with very low production costs. This ideology is that oil and gas is not the ultimate goal – it's all about control. Remember the movie "Three Days of the Condor" with Robert Redford?

The Caspian Sea has major reserves near former Soviet republics including Kazakhstan. These Russian states may have up to three times the reserves of the U.S., second only to the Persian Gulf region. Multinationals are pursuing these trillions of dollars in reserves with their main concern being the politics of the region, and the strategies for transportation of the oil. Kazakhstan's offshore Kashagan field is gigantic. Still, the oil has to be shipped across the Caspian Sea to Baku. The Baku-Tbilis-Ceyhan pipeline is a 1,099 mile long crude oil pipeline from the Caspian to the Mediterranean Sea. It connects Baku, the capital of Azerbaijan; Tbilisi, the capital of Georgia, and Ceyhan, a Turkish port.

Discovered in July 2000, Kashagan has been described as the largest field found in the past 30 years, the largest outside the Middle East and with projected output close to that of the Ghawar field in Saudi Arabia. It is being developed by a group of partners including Shell, Exxon Mobil, Total, ConocoPhilips and Kazahk state-run oil company KazMunaiGas.

Russia is a large producer of oil and has significant market share. The Russian economy is quite sensitive to oil prices – in the last few months, as crude has dropped below $ 50 a barrel, this has greatly impacted Russia. In order to balance the federal budget, Russia needs at least $ 70 per barrel. Russian oil production costs average nearly $ 10 per barrel, some of the highest in the world. Economic and political stability in Russia are both threatened. Russia has a self-interest in higher oil prices. The Russian ruble has suffered a variety of devaluations. Some analysts say that Saudi Arabia and the U.S. have conspired to produce this low per-barrel price in order to sanction the Russians. If so, this is insane since it could lead to World War III – economic sanctions have preceded every other war in history!

The James Baker III Institute for Public Policy published a paper entitled 'Vladimir Putin and the Geopolitics of Oil.' It's interesting to observe what is currently happening, and this will serve as a lesson text to investors and potential investors. As profile information, Michael Khodorkovsky is the wealthiest man in Russia, and the 16th wealthiest man in the world, due primarily to his holding in the Russian petroleum company Yukos. On October 25th, 2003, he was arrested at gunpoint on a Siberian airport runway by the Russian prosecutor general's office, on charges of tax evasion. Shortly thereafter, on October 31st, the government further took the unprecedented step of freezing shares of Yukos due to tax charges. Moscow has produced some of wealthiest men in the world, one of them buying an estate in the south of France not long ago for $ 800 Million. Russia's oligarchs have risen to wealth only recently. To give credit to Vladimir Putin, it must be mentioned that Khodorkovsky's associates were arrested several months ahead of him, and this gave him ample chance to leave the country with fair warning, which Khodorkovsky did not heed.

From the study:

The honeymoon between the Western oil industry and Russian President Vladimir Putin ended in mid-2003 when the Russian procurator's office began arresting Yukos executives. The arrest of Yukos CEO Mikhail Khodorkovsky triggered speculation that conditions in Russia are becoming less favorable to investors, as it came at a time when Yukos' principle owners and managers were engaged in merger talks with senior executives from ChevronTexaco and ExxonMobil.

Signs of this shift were visible even before the presidential elections. In January 2004, the Russian government announced that it wanted over $ 1 billion for a license to explore and develop one of the three Sakhalin-3 parcels, the choice Kirinsky block, the rights to which would be won through a tender process. The decision effectively annulled the results of a 1993 tender. It was a particular blow to ExxonMobil, which had already invested over $ 80 million in the project and had been withholding further investment in the project in the hopes of being able to develop it through a production-sharing agreement.

As intended, the arrest and subsequent treatment of Khodorkovsky had almost theatrical quality from the onset (theatrical at least for those watching from the outside-certainly not for the figure at the center of the drama). In the early morning hours of October 25, 2003, approximately twenty armed, black-uniformed agents boarded Khodorkovsky's private jet and arrested him. Khodorkovsky was put in a cell with five other inmates at the Matrosskaya Tishina pre-trial detention facility.

Putin accurately assessed that Khodorkovsky is not a man who accepts defeat. Khodorkovsky preferred jail to exile, as in the months before his arrest there were clear signals from Kremlin circles that leaving Russia permanently was a prudent option.

President Putin believes that Russian ownership of Russia's resource base is critical to Russia's economic recovery and to the country's reemergence as an important international actor. Putin does not believe in relying on global market forces to provide the economic opportunities and social supports necessary for the Russian people to make a successful transition from communist rule to a modern, European-style economy and political system. Putin has given a lot of thought to these questions.

Putin wrote a candidate of science dissertation on the topic of 'Mineral Raw Materials in the Strategy for Development of the Russian Economy' at St. Petersburg's prestigious State Mining Institute. He knows the field. In this article he argues that development of the natural resource base will serve as a guarantor of the country's international position.

With this in mind, let's see what would happen with a Mideast war. The Strait of Hormuz is of great strategic importance, as it is the only sea route through which oil from Kuwait, Iraq, Iran, Saudi Arabia, Bahrain, Qatar as well as United Arab Emirates can be transported. It touches Iran to the north and Oman to the South. Its width is only 50 km at its narrowest point. Iran would likely block this route if attacked, prohibiting the transport of OPEC oil from that point forwards. The futures market would react with large swings in crude, probably to over $ 200 per barrel in short order, as it would close down a substantial percentage of the world's oil.

The Global War On Terrorism (GWOT) is the pretext to this theater war. Both the level of naval power, as well as the level of threat, are at unprecedented levels.

A naval blockade by close to 80 ships is tantamount to a declaration of war.

A new unit JFCCSGS was created a few years ago: Joint Functional Component Command Space and Global Strike. It has the mandate to oversee the launching of a nuclear attack in accordance with the 2002 Nuclear Posture Review, approved by US Congress in 2002. The NPR underscores the pre-emptive use of nuclear warheads against "rogue states" and also China and Russia.

Under the NATO Transatlantic Partnership Document, US and allied forces including Israel would "resort to a pre-emptive nuclear attack to try to halt the imminent spread of nuclear weapons." (quote from Sidney Morning Herald).

According to a 2003 Senate decision, tactical nukes are "harmless to the civilian population" since they are detonated underground, though they can range up to six times as powerful as the Hiroshima explosion.

Fast forward to today:

Lithuanian President Dalia Grybauskaite even claimed that Russia is effectively waging war against all of Europe.

"It is the fact that Russia is in a war state against Ukraine. That means it is in a state of war against a country which would like to be closely integrated with the EU. Practically Russia is in a state of war against Europe," she said.

What few in the West, outside a handful of military experts grasp, however, is that the US project to install so-called Ballistic Missile Defense missiles and special radar in Poland, the Czech Republic, Turkey and Bulgaria is a highly provocative act by Washington against Russia and risks putting the world on a hair-trigger to a nuclear war. Putin has threatened to destroy the missile sites.

Lord Stirling, a military consultant, has stated:

Sometime in the years ahead, there will be a war launched against Iran. The war may be started by Israel, or by the United States, or by a NATO/EU/US embargo, or by some 'false flag' attack. What matters is that it will begin; and where it will take the world.

Regardless if the war begins with a limited number of air strikes against Iranian military and nuclear targets, or if an all-out several thousand target attack begins from day one, the probabilities of the war becoming a major regional war within 48 hours are 90% or higher.

The Iranians will simply not allow Israeli and/or American military forces to attack its territory without a major response. Any significant counter-attack on Israel and/or American regional bases will trigger a much greater counter-response.

The Iranians have equipped, paid for, and trained a massive unguided rocket and guided missile force in Lebanon (the largest such force in human history). These missiles are in place as a MAD force (a MAD ~ mutually assured destruction ~ force is one that is a doomsday force; established to prevent the use of overwhelming military force by allowing a return "punch" of overwhelming military destructive force upon one's enemy). The total number of missiles and rockets in Lebanon are variously estimated at between 40,000 and 110,000. While many are unguided Katyusha rockets, many are longer ranged guided missiles. All are operated by Hezbollah Special Forces launch teams.

The Hezbollah Special Forces are in effect a highly trained and well-equipped Iranian commando force of at least a Brigade in size. They man and protect a large number of mostly unguided and rather crude rockets, generally Katyusha 122mm artillery rockets with a 19 mile/30km range and capable of delivering approximately 66 pounds/30kg of warheads. Additionally, Hezbollah are known to possess a considerable number of more advanced and longer range missiles. During the 2006 war Hezbollah fired approximately 4,000 rockets (95% of which were Katyushas) all utilizing only "dumb" high explosive warheads. Some Iranian-built and supplied Fajr-3 and Ra'ad 1 liquid-fueled missiles were also fired. It is believed that the larger and longer range missiles are directly under the control of Syrian and Iranian officers.

The combination of short to medium range rockets and guided missiles in Lebanon, and the longer range guided missiles in Syria, the smaller number of rockets and missiles in the West Bank and Gaza, and the longer range guided missiles in Iran present a massive throw weight of warheads aimed at Israel.

It now appears that Israel has given up on the idea of a ground assault to remove the many rocket and missile launchers in Lebanon. A senior Israeli general has resigned with the complaint that the Army is not training sufficiently to fight in Lebanon. The alternative is the use of FAE (fuel air explosive) technology weapons and neutron bombs (a type of nuclear weapon that produces a higher short-term radiological output and less blast output than normal nuclear weapons).

Any use of such WMD by the Israeli Army on the Hezbollah forces in Lebanon will likely automatically trigger the use of WMD warheads on whatever rockets/missiles remain operational (if their use has not already been authorized due to the nature and scope of Israeli and/or American attacks on Iran).

The bottom line of this is that Israel will face a truly massive number of rockets and missiles from Lebanon warheads. Additionally, a sizable number of such weapons/warheads will be fired from Gaza and the West Bank. The Syrians will be using larger, more accurate guided missiles to shower WMD upon Israel as will the Iranians. To counter this, the Israelis will be using their Israeli and American anti-missile missiles. They will have good success in knocking down many incoming missiles but the sheer number of incoming weapons could overload many defensive measures.

By *intentionally* giving the presidency to an apocalyptically-minded, anti-semitic extremist who threatened to destroy Israel after taking office and then *intentionally* letting the IAEA and West know that an atomic bomb is being built, apparently sooner than later, Teheran is provoking Israel and/or the U.S. into preemptively attacking. This, I would dare say, *IS the intent*. Iran is baiting Israel and America to take military action against its nuclear facilities. If Teheran's intention was to complete building an atomic bomb, then it should have discretely continued clandestine efforts to do so rather than announcing to the world it's capabilities and intentions such that Israel and/or the U.S. militarily eliminate the developing threat. The course that Iran has chosen to follow seems geared to provoke an attack more so than to actually complete development of a nuclear weapon.

Putin of Russia has publicly stated that if the US assists Israel in attacking Iran, or if we attack Iran, he would attack America.

Strangely, in helping Iran develop nuclear and ballistic missile weaponry, Russia is seemingly acting against its own national interests. Iran, an extremist state, has long been known as a sponsor of international terrorism. Russia, stemming from its war in Chechnya, has purportedly been a repeat victim of Islamic terrorists (although some question the true source of terrorism against Russia). Hence, it seems to make little sense that Russia is helping to provide the world's ultimate Islamic extremist state with the means by which to build and launch nuclear bombs as far as Moscow. Yet, this is how history is unfolding. Could it be that Russia doesn't feel threatened by the Islamic radicals in Teheran?

If not, why? I leave conclusions to the reader. Cutting edge news offers more insight into the plans being made in the Mideast.

A Russian general's statement about Iran's nukes failed to register with media a few years ago. Sometimes a slip of the tongue is so incredible that no amount of doctoring can explain it. And sometimes a slip of the tongue is as intentional as could be. Take an appearance by Russian Deputy Chief of Staff Gen. Yuri Baluyevsky. He gave a briefing in Moscow during a Bush-Putin summit and was asked about whether Iran actually fired the Shihab-3 intermediate-range missile in a successful test. The second question was whether Iran can threaten Israel, Russia or the United States with its nuclear and missile programs.

Then the Russian general takes a surprise turn: "Now, as to whether or not Iran has tested something like that. Iran does have nuclear weapons,' Baluyevsky said. 'Of course, these are non-strategic nuclear weapons. I mean these are not ICBMs with a range of more than 5,500 kilometers and more."

Now this is shocking news, indeed! This Russian general has just confirmed that Iran has nuclear warheads and theater missiles with which to deliver them! And, he seems not to be concerned because these warheads cannot yet hit Russian soil. If Iran has nuclear weapons and the missile capability with which to deliver them to Israeli targets, then the entire calculation of military balance in the Middle East may just have changed.

I believe this indicates a very high measure of alarm issued on an international geo-political basis. This is a reason we should place energy and gold investments as a very critical part of our portfolio.

Bibliography

Kashagan, Caspian Sea, Kazakhstan, Article in Offshore Technology, http://www.offshore-technology.com/projects/kashagan/

Olcott, Dr. Martha Brill, The Energy Dimension in Russian Global Strategy – Vladimir Putin and the Geopolitics of Oil, The James A. Baker III Institute for Public Policy of Rice University, 2004

Commander, U.S. 2nd Fleet Public Affairs, "Operation Brimstone" Flexes Allied Force Training, *http://www.navy.mil/search/display.asp?story_id=38478*

Stirling, Lord, War on Iran – The Perfect Storm, *http://europebusines.blogspot.com/*

Adams, J. Is Iran Trying To Start World War Three? *http://www.spiritoftruth.org/iraniannuclearbomb.htm*

Stratfor Intelligence, Russian General Confirms Iran Has Nuclear Weapons, *http://cuttingedge.org/news/n1660.cfm*

ESSENTIAL KNOWLEDGE

"Of course the gold and silver markets are manipulated. You have to be either blind or a Harvard Graduate with a doctorate in Economics to ignore the fact." Hugo Salinas Price

Note: Market conditions tend to change continuously, and so do recommendations. However, I believe you'll get solid advice and service from this reliable source, who has kindly contributed this Article that follows:

http://the-moneychanger.com/

They do gold and silver brokerage and are highly recommended.

Franklin Sanders
The Moneychanger
PO Box 178
Westpoint, TN 38486
888)218-9226

Here is the Article in its entirety.

1. **Always take delivery.**
2. **Never buy premium if you can avoid it.**
3. **Buy bullion for business, numismatics for fun.**
4. **Buy silver first, then gold.**
5. **Buy small gold first, then large.**
6. **Never buy exotic coins or modern rarities or anything you don't understand.**
7. **Know your dealer.**
8. **What governments can't find, they can't steal.**
9. **Never swap bullion coins for U.S. $20 gold pieces.**
10. **Never break the law.**

Please note that our recommendations vary depending on your concerns and the market. If you want to invest in gold and silver to protect your assets and have something easily divisible and spend-able to hedge currency depreciation or collapse, then:

- **If you have $5,000 or less to spend**
  At least half in silver (either US 90% silver coin or 1oz. Silver Rounds) and half in British Sovereigns, French 20 Francs, Mexican Pesos (10, 5, 2.5 or 2) or some other inexpensive, fractional gold coin.

- **For $10,000 buy**
  Two-thirds US 90% silver coin or 1oz. Silver Rounds, with the balance divided between a fractional coin like British Sovereigns, French 20 Francs, Mexican Pesos (10, 5, 2.5, or 2) AND Krugerrands, Austrian 100 Coronas or Mexican 50 Pesos.

- **For $25,000 buy**
  Two-thirds US 90% silver coin or 1oz. Silver Rounds; half of the remaining third in Sovereigns, French 20 Francs, or 1/4 oz. American Eagles; and the balance in one oz. Krugerrands, Austrian 100 Coronas, Mexican 50 Pesos, or American Eagles.

- **For $75,000 buy**
  Two-thirds US 90% silver coin or 1oz. Silver Rounds; $5,000 worth of Sovereigns, 20 Francs, or 1/4 Eagles; the balance in Krugerrands, American Eagles, Mexican 50 Pesos or Austrian 100 Coronas. (For over $75,000 simply do multiples of this portfolio.)

If you want to invest in precious metals to simply protect your assets and don't think you'll ever need to actually barter with them, then:

- **If you have $5,000 or less to spend**
  Half in US 90% silver coin or 1oz. Silver Rounds, half in one ounce Krugerrands or American Eagles, Austrian 100 Coronas, or Mexican 50 Pesos.

- **For $5,000 through $25,000**

    Put at least half of your money in US 90% silver coin or 1oz. Silver Rounds; the rest in one ounce Krugerrands or American Eagles, or in Austrian 100 Coronas or Mexican 50 Pesos.

- **For $75,000**

    Get bags of US 90% silver or 1oz. Silver Rounds for 2/3 of your order; the balance in Krugerrands, American Eagles, 100 Coronas, or 50 Pesos. (For over $75,000 simply do multiples of this portfolio.)

What is the US 90% silver coin and why do you recommend it?

90% silver coin is quarters, dimes, and half-dollars minted before 1965. (90% silver coin does *not* include silver dollars.) Everyone knows that 4 quarters = 1 dollar. In the same way, 4 quarters minted before 1965 = 1 face value dollar. A face value dollar is how we sell 90% silver coin. So, when you ask for the price of 90% silver we will say it costs, for example, $25.00 per face value dollar. A face value dollar is either 10 dimes, four quarters, or two half-dollars. A face value dollar contains .715 ounces of silver. The standard trading unit for 90% silver coin is a "bag" of $1,000.00 face value, containing 715 troy ounces. You can purchase any portion of a bag that you wish. We recommend 90% silver coin simply because it is often the cheapest, most divisible, most widely recognized and traded form of silver.

What about silver rounds, what are those?

Silver rounds are simply one ounce, 99.9% pure silver coins minted in the United States. They are made by various private refineries and are *not* just round "blanks" of silver. They all have varying pictures because the companies that mint them have varying production runs using different designs. Regardless of the picture on their front and back, all silver rounds we sell state clearly on their face, "1oz. silver, 99.9% pure (or .999 fine)." We sometimes recommend silver rounds instead of 90% silver coin because premiums (not our commission—the premium is the percentage over the spot price that you pay for a coin) on both coins fluctuate for a variety of reasons. Since we consider it our duty to sell you liquid coins for the best price, sometimes our recommendations change.

Why do you recommend gold coins like Krugerrands, Austrian 100 Coronas, and Mexican 50 Pesos, and what are they?

We recommend these foreign coins because they cost less per ounce and give you more gold for your money than the American Eagle gold coin series (which is minted in the United States today). All of these coins are well known in the industry and any dealer will readily buy them. The 22 karat South African Krugerrand gold coin contains exactly one troy ounce of fine (pure) gold. The American Eagle copied the Krugerrand's specifications, and is minted to exactly the same weight and fineness. The Austrian 100 Coronae is an official re-strike from the Austrian mint. It is 20 karat (90% pure) and contains exactly 0.9802 troy ounce fine gold. The Mexican 50 Peso is an official re-strike from the 400-year old Mexico City mint. A 20 karat coin, it contains exactly 1.2057 troy ounce of fine gold. These three coins take turns as the cheapest on our price sheet.

What about the purity of the Krugerrand, Eagle, 50 Peso, and Austrian 100 Coronae? Will they be worth less later since they're not 24 karat?

Purity is largely irrelevant among gold and silver dealers. Coins and bars are bought and sold based on their weight, not their purity. Unless you're going to melt the coins down, it's just not an issue and doesn't affect the price.

Why do you recommend older-issue, foreign fractional gold coins instead of modern issues or American Eagle fractionals?

Modern issues like American Eagles, Maple Leaves, Philharmonics, and Nuggets include half, quarter, and tenth ounce coins: the smaller the coin, the higher the cost per ounce. With the smallest coins, premiums over the gold content approach 15%. That makes no economic sense because gold is gold. British sovereigns (containing 0.2354 troy ounce fine gold), French 20 francs (0.1867 oz.), Swiss 20 francs (0.1867 oz.), German 20 marks (0.2304 oz.), Netherlands 10 guilders (0.1947 oz.), the whole series of Mexican peso coins, and a number of other gold coins offer lower cost per ounce and good liquidity. Not recommended are gold coins so infrequently seen in this country that you will suffer a big discount when you sell them, such as Iranian pahlavis (0.2354 oz.) or Saudi guineas (0.2354 oz.). If you can't sell them, they're not a bargain.

Nowhere in your recommendations do I see anything about pure gold coins like the Canadian Maple Leaf or Austrian Philharmonic. Why not?

Gold is one of the softest and most ductile metals. Pure gold coins scratch and scar very easily unless handled with extreme care. Throughout history gold coins have generally been alloyed with copper or silver, hardening them to withstand circulation. Customers often unwittingly damage pure gold coins and therefore receive up to 5% less for them when they sell. In our opinion the purity of 24 karat gold confers no benefit and in fact often creates drawbacks.

What is reported when I buy or sell gold or silver?

Everything is exempt from reporting **when you buy** gold or silver, unless you pay more than $10,000 in cash. Even then it's not your gold or silver purchase that must be reported, only the cash transaction. Contrary to the scare stories, very few things are reportable **when you sell**. Under 26 CFR 1.6045-1 and Rev.Proc. 92-103, dealers need only report customer sales of 25 or more (but not fewer) Krugerrands, Maple Leaves, or Mexican Onzas, five bag lots ($5,000 face value} of US 90% silver coin, kilo gold bars, 100 oz. gold bars, 1,000 oz. silver bars, or 50 oz. or 100 oz. of platinum. If you sell lots smaller than these, the dealer reports nothing.

What about government gold confiscation?

We expect it more likely for you to be abducted by aliens than for the Federal Government to attempt gold confiscation. First, gold no longer forms a significant part of the monetary reserves in this country, as it did in 1934 and therefore, confiscation makes no sense. Second, the folks who tell you about government confiscation are generally trying to sell you overpriced coins that will line their pockets and empty yours. For more information, read our article on numismatics:

http://the-moneychanger.com/answers/what_is_a_numismatic_coin

Courtesy of Franklin Sanders:

http://the-moneychanger.com/answers/ten_commandments_for_buying_gold_and_silver

EXECUTING A PLAN

"A good plan violently executed today is better than a perfect plan executed tomorrow." – GEORGE PATTON

By: The Gold Report – note – this interview is courtesy of the *Gold Report*, and it's several years old, but it's the best one in recent history in my opinion, and gives us much macroeconomic data about how to use Gold Stocks in our portfolios. The strategies and key principles are all contained right here.

Heralded as "the best of today's best," John Doody, author and publisher of the highly regarded Gold Stock Analyst newsletter, brings a unique perspective to gold stock analysis. In this exclusive interview with The Gold Report, Doody ponders the efficacy of the Keynesian approach, makes a case for gold equities and explains how the GSA Top 10 Stocks portfolio has outperformed every other gold investment vehicle since 1994.

The Gold Report: John, you've stated in your newsletter, Gold Stock Analyst: "It's clear the U.S. is going down a Keynesian approach to get out of this recession/depression." I am curious on your viewpoint. Will the Keynesian approach actually work, or will they need to eventually move over to the Chicago School of Free Markets?

John Doody: A free market approach of letting the crisis resolve itself would work, but would cause too much damage; we'd probably lose our auto industry, and it would take too much time. As Keynes said: "In the long run we're all dead," so the government is trying to get a faster resolution. The Treasury is pursuing his fiscal policy idea of deficit spending. They're borrowing the money to bail out the banks.

Bernanke and the Fed are pursuing a loose monetary policy with a now 0% interest rate. There's actually no way we can not end up with inflation. This is much bigger than 'The New Deal' under Roosevelt. And I think that the market disarray over the last several months has confused investors; but when the markets settle down, it's clear to me that it will be up for gold and gold stocks.

TGR: Is there any economic scenario that you wouldn't see gold going up in?

JD: Basically, we're pumping money into the system, but it's just sitting there. It's not being put to work, so there are those who think that we are going to enter a deflationary era. But I can't see that. Some don't like Bernanke, but I think there's probably nobody better prepared to be in his role.

Bernanke is a student of the Great Depression and knows the mistakes the Fed made then, such as forcing banks to upgrade the quality of loans on their balance sheets. His approach is to buy the banks' low quality loans, enabling them to make new loans. They haven't done much of the latter yet, which is probably a fault of the Fed not requiring the funds received for the junk to be redeployed, but they ultimately will lend more as that's how banks make money.

He knows in the early 1930s we went into a deflationary period of falling prices. For three or four years prices were down about 10% annually. He fully understands the risks of that, one of which is the increased burden of existing debt payments on falling incomes. The debt burden is lighter in an inflationary environment and that's his target. Long term, he knows he can cure inflation; Volker showed us how with high interest rates in the 1980s. But there's no sure way to cure deflation, and so Bernanke's doing everything possible to avoid a falling price level. And I think that, because this is a service-driven economy, companies won't lower prices to sell more goods—they will just lay off more workers, as we're seeing now. I don't think we'll get the price deflation of the '30s, and I'm sure Bernanke is going to do everything to prevent it.

TGR: But aren't we already in a deflationary period?

JD: Well, we may be to an extent; you can get a better buy on a car. But, to put it in the simplest terms, has your yard guy lowered his price, or your pool guy, or even your webmaster?

TGR: Yes, but people opt to do things themselves versus paying other people to do it.

JD: Maybe, but if they do, it won't show up in prices—it will show up in the unemployment statistics. So if the yard guy, pool guy or webmaster don't lower prices and their clients become do-it-yourselfers, the effect will show up in unemployment, not inflation data.

TGR: So if every major country in the world is increasing their monetary supply, we would expect inflation. Will there be any currency that comes out of this to be considered the new base currency, sort of like the U.S. dollar is now?

JD: Well, that's the $64,000 question. We don't really know and, because there's no totally obvious currency, that is why the dollar is doing well of late. But the dollar is in a long-term downtrend, in part because interest rates in Europe remain higher than here. Higher interest rates, as you know, act like a magnet in attracting investment money, which first has to be converted to the higher interest currency and that bids up its value versus the dollar.

The Euro represents an economy about the size of the U.S., so there may be some safety there. You could argue for the Swiss Franc maybe, but you know the Swiss banks (Credit Suisse, for example) have had some problems, so we're not quite sure how that's going.

So, to me, the only clear money that's going to survive all this and go up, because everything else is going to go down, is gold.

TGR: What's your view of holding physical gold versus gold equities?

JD: I only hold gold equities. They're more readily tradable; when gold goes up, the equities tend to go up by a factor of two or three times. Of course, that works to the reverse, as we know. As gold went down, the equities went down more. But because you hold them in a government-guaranteed SIPC account, it provides ease of trading—you don't have the worries of physical gold. . .insurance, storage or whatever. You may want to hold a few coins, but that would be about it in my opinion.

TGR: On your website, your approach to investing in gold equities is to choose a portfolio of 10 companies that have the opportunity to double in an 18- to 24-month period with the current gold price.

JD: Yes. We don't really look forward more than 18 or 24 months; but within that timeframe, say a year from now, we could reassess and raise our targets so that, in the following 18 to 24 months, the stocks, while having gone up, could go up more still. There are lots of opportunities to stay in the same stocks as long as they continue to perform well. We're not a trading newsletter, and as you probably know, the way we define an undervalued stock is based on two metrics.

One is market cap per ounce. The market capitalization of a company is the number of shares times its price. You divide that by its ounces of production and its ounces of proven and probable reserves, and you see how the company's data compares to the industry's weighted averages.

Second, we look at operating cash flow multiples. Take the difference between the gold price and the cash cost to produce an ounce, multiply that by the company's production per year, and you get operating cash flow. Divide that into its market capitalization and you get its operating cash flow multiple. We look at that this much the same as one looks at earnings per share multiples in other industries.

For reference, we last calculated the industry averages on December 29, 2008 for the 50+ gold miners we follow, which is everyone of significance. At that time, the average market cap for an ounce of production was $3,634, an ounce of proven and probable reserves was $194, and the average operating cash flow multiple on forecast 2009 production, assuming $900/oz gold, was 7.4X.

We focus on companies that are below the averages and try to figure out why. An ounce of gold is an ounce of gold, it doesn't matter who mined it. If you're going to buy an ounce of gold from a coin dealer, you want to get the cheapest price. Well, if you're going to buy an ounce of gold in the stock market, you should want to get those at the cheapest price, too. It's oversimplified, as there are other factors to be considered, but this is a primary screening tool to determine which stocks merit further study. The method works, as the GSA Top 10 Stocks portfolio has outperformed every other gold investment vehicle since we began in 1994.

TGR: Are all the companies in your coverage producers?

JD: Yes, all are producing or near-producing. They may be in the money-raising stage to build a mine, but they've got an independently determined reserve. And that part of the market has done better than the explorers because it has more data to underpin the stocks' prices.

TGR: And you focus in on having 10 just because, as you point out in your materials, it allows you to maximum upside at minimum risk (i.e., if one of the 10 goes down 50%, you will only lose 5% of your money). Is your portfolio always at 10 or does it ever expand more than that?

JD: No, earlier in 2008 we were 40% cash, so it was six stocks. For a couple of months later in 2008 it was 11 stocks. But 90% of the time it's at 10.

TGR: What prompted you to be 40% in cash?

JD: That was when Bear Stearns was rescued in March and gold went to $1000; we were just uncomfortable with that whole scenario. And actually we put the 40% in the gold ETF; so it wasn't true cash.

TGR: Okay. And as you're looking at these undervalued companies, are you finding that there are certain qualifications? Are they typically in a certain area, certain size?

JD: While we follow Barrick Gold Corporation (NYSE:ABX) and Newmont Mining Corp. (NYSE:NEM) and they've both been Top 10 in the past, neither is now. We're currently looking further down the food chain. There's one with over two million ounces growing to four million a year. Another has a million growing to two million. So, some are still pretty good sized. And then there are others further down that are either developing mines or are very cheap on a market cap per ounce basis.

Earlier, one of the Top 10 was selling at its "cash in the bank" price. We've had a nice little rally since October and this stock has doubled, but it's still cheap. It has 9 million ounces of reserves at three mine sites in European Community nations, and it's not Gabriel in Romania. It has no major troubles with permitting its mines and it was selling at its cash/share. Then the chairman of the board bought 5 million more shares. It was already top 10, but I pointed this out to subscribers as great buy signal. It's doubled since and will double again, in our opinion.

TGR: Can you share with us some of the ones that are in your top 10?

JD: Well, the astute investor would probably recognize Goldcorp (TSX:G) (NYSE:GG) as the one at two million ounces growing to four million ounces. Their tremendous new mine in Mexico, Penasquito, which I have been to and written about, is going to average half a million ounces of gold and 30 million ounces of silver a year. **It's going to be the biggest producing silver mine in the world, momentarily anyway, and will produce huge quantities of lead and zinc.** At current prices, it's going to be a billion-dollar-a-year revenues mine, which is enormous. And because of by-products, and even at current prices, the 500,000 ounces of gold per year will be produced at a negative cash cost per ounce.

TGR: Wow. Because of the credits?

JD: Because of the by-product credits. Another one would be Yamana Gold Inc. (NYSE:AUY), which is growing from a million ounces to two million ounces. Both Yamana and Goldcorp are in politically safe areas—no Bolivia, no Ecuador, no Romania—none of the places where you have to take political risk. I think we've learned enough from the Crystallex International Corp. (KRY) and Gold Reserve Inc. (TSX:GRZ) (NYSE:GRZ) situation in Venezuela, where they're both on portions of the same huge deposit that is probably 25 million ounces or more. It looks to me that the government is going to take it away from them. So, I would just as soon not be involved in that kind of political risk scenario. There's enough risk in gold just from the mining aspects of it that you don't have to take chances on the politics too, as in some nations that's impossible to assess.

TGR: Yes, another one that is really doing quite well is Royal Gold Inc. (Nasdaq:RGLD). Can you speak about that company?

JD: Yes. Royal Gold has been GSA Top 10 for 18 months now. We put it on in part because of the Penasquito deposit that I mentioned earlier. Royal has a 2% royalty on that, and 2% of a billion dollars is $20 million a year. Royal is unique in that they haven't prostituted themselves by selling shares on a continuous basis. They only have 34 million shares outstanding and they will have royalty income this year of about $100 million. Penasquito is just coming on line, so its $20 million per year won't be fully seen until late 2010.

Plus Royal pays a dividend. I think it could pay $1.00/share ($0.32 now). Dividend-paying gold stocks typically trade at a 1% yield. A $1.00/share dividend would make Royal a potential $100 stock. That's my crystal ball down-the-road target.

Royal is a great play on gold price because they don't have the aggravation of mining. They have a portfolio of mine royalties, plus a small corporate office. Royal employs 16 people, has $150 million in the bank and over $100 million a year income, which is about $3.00 per share pre-tax. Their biggest cost is taxes.

TGR: I see also that Franco Nevada Corp. (FNV.TO) has had quite a rise, though they have been kind of tumultuous between November and December.

JD: Franco is also a stock we like. About half of its royalties are from oil, so that's why it's suffered. The original Franco Nevada, as you know, was merged into Newmont for five years, and then they came public again in December '07. I think it's a good way to play gold and oil, and I think everybody agrees that oil is not going to stay in the $40 range for long.

TGR: John, can you give us a few more?

JD: A couple of smaller ones we like are Northgate Minerals Corp. (TSX:NGX) (AMEX:NXG) and Golden Star Resources Ltd. (TSX:GSC) . Northgate is a misunderstood producer. Everybody thinks it's going out of business when the Kemess Mine closes after 2011, but it's actually not. It has 200,000 ounces a year from two mines in Australia and has a potential new mine in Ontario where they've just announced over three million ounces. That's potentially another 200,000 ounces a year, so we think they'll remain at 400,000 ounces a year from Canada and Australia, both of which are countries we like. Cheap on our market cap per ounce of production and reserves metrics, it's trading at an operating cash flow multiple under 2.0X.

Golden Star has several nearby mines in Ghana with production targeted at about 500,000 ounces in 2009. They've been ramping up to this rate for the past year and cash costs have run much higher than plan. If costs can be controlled and production goals met, it's a takeover candidate for someone already in the country, such as Newmont or Gold Fields Ltd. (NYSE:GFI) (JSE:GFI) .

One thing I think readers should bear in mind is that gold mining will be one of the few industries doing well in 2009. Their key cost is oil, which is about 25% of the cost of running a mine. Oil's price, as we know, is down about 75% in the $147/barrel high last July. At the average $400 cash cost per ounce mine, that's a cut of about $75/oz off their costs. That result alone is going to give them an uptick in future earnings versus what they showed for third quarter 2008.

Something else people may not recognize is that currencies are also falling; many are down 20% to 40% versus the U.S. dollar. All the commodity nation currencies—the Canadian dollar, the Australian dollar, the South African Rand, the Brazilian Real, the Mexican Peso—they're all down 20% to 40%. When your mining costs in those countries are translated back into U.S. dollars, they'll be 20% to 40% lower.

So, the miners are going to have falling cash costs and even if the gold price remains exactly where it is now profits are going to soar. This will be unique in 2009. I can't think of any other industry in which people are going to be able to point to and say, "These guys are making a lot more money." I think the increasing profits will get the gold mining industry recognition that it isn't getting now. Of course I'm a bull on gold because of the macroeconomic picture. When you put falling costs of production together with a rising gold price, you've got a winning combination for the stocks in 2009.

TGR: I was wondering if you could give us something on Silver Wheaton Corp. (NYSE:SLW) (TSX:SLW) .

JD: Well, **Silver Wheaton is another royalty company**; it's not a producer. It gets its profit royalties by paying a cash sum up front and $4/ounce on an ongoing basis. It captures the difference between the silver price and $4 an ounce; if silver is $10 and it pays $4, it makes a $6 an ounce profit; at $20 silver, its profit would be $16. Aside from no pure silver miner actually producing ounces as low as $4.00, there's a lot of leverage to silver price. I am not a silver bull, but because I'm a gold bull I think silver will follow gold higher.

Silver Wheaton is one of those companies that doesn't have the issues of actually doing the mining. It has a portfolio of mines that it gets production from, and it owns 25% of the production from Goldcorp's Penasquito mine that it buys at $4 an ounce, and will average about 8 million ounces a year.

It's just starting up now, but it will really get going in 2010. Silver Wheaton's share of the total mineralization at Penasquito is 1 billion ounces. There's 4 billion total ounces of silver there and it bought 25%. So, for a long time—the mine life of Penasquito is over 30 years—it's going to be a big producing mine for Silver Wheaton.

TGR: Isn't there a twin sister to Silver Wheaton in the gold area?

JD: Well, there's Gold Wheaton Gold Corp. (TSX.V:GLW). It's based on the premise that some companies have a gold by-product. With their primary production in some other kind of metal, some might like to lay off the gold for a $400 an ounce on-going payment and an up-front purchase amount. Yes, some of the same guys are involved. I'm not convinced it's going to do as well because it's already got a lot of shares outstanding, and I just don't like the capital structure as much. I wouldn't bet against these guys but I'm not a believer.

TGR: And you said you're not a silver bull. Why is that?

JD: We do cover about 15 silver miners, but reason number one for not being a bull is that it's a by-product. Few mines are built to get just silver; 70% to 80% of silver comes as a by-product to copper, zinc, gold or some other metal. If you're producing copper, you're more interested in the copper price than you are in the silver price and you tend to just dump the silver onto the market.

And second, it's not a monetary commodity. It is poor man's gold—but it doesn't have the universal monetary acceptance that gold does. It has a growing list of industrial uses, but it's not growing at any rate that's going to offset the falling use in photography. So, the overall demand for silver is not growing at any great rate. It's not going to go from 800 million ounces a year to 1.6 billion ounces a year; it may get there in 20 years or 30 years, but that's not our investment time horizon.

I think silver just follows gold along; but, in fact, it hasn't been following gold along because right now silver is trading at a discount to gold. The ratio of gold to silver price, which normally runs around 50–55, is now around 80, so silver might have a little bit of a pop-up if the discount closes. But there are a lot of new silver mines coming on line and maybe that's why the discount exists. Penasquito is one and Silver Standard Resources Inc. (TSX.:SSO) (Nasdaq:SSRI) has a big one starting in 2009. Coeur d'Alene Mines Corp. (NYSE:CDE) (TSX: CDM) has now one ramping up and Apex Silver Mines Ltd. (AMEX:SIL) San Cristobal is now on line at 20+ million ounces per year as a zinc by-product. There's potentially more silver coming to market than the world really needs. We do recommend Silver Wheaton, but that's our single play.

TGR: Can you give us any comments on Minefinders Corporation (AMEX:MFN) (MFL.TO) ?

JD: Well, you know, it's in the uncertainty phase as to whether or not the new Delores mine in Mexico is going to work. Now built, it's just starting up. We like the stock as we think it's going to work. The question is: will it? Two mines in the area—Mulatos, owned by Alamos Gold Inc. (TSX:AGI) , and Ocampo owned by Gammon Gold Inc. (GRS) did not start up smoothly. The market is betting against Delores starting smoothly, but this is the last of the three mines to come on line, and the first two mines—Alamos' and Gammon's—did get fixed and are now running okay. So, I think Minefinders has probably learned from the experience of the others, and the mine should start up all right. But, you know, the proof will be in the pudding. If you take its market cap per ounce on the forecast 185,000 ounces of production in 2009, or its almost 5 million ounces of reserves, and compare it to the industry averages we calculate, it's potentially a double or triple from here.

TGR: So, the start-up issues of the other two mines, were they politically related?

JD: No, it was metal related. Processing facilities aren't like televisions; you don't just turn them on. It's more like buying a new fancy computer system that needs to be twiddled and tweaked and loaded with the right programs. And you know, all geology is different, so things seldom start up properly;

and, given the long teething problems at the other two mines, that's sort of been a curse. If Minefinders can beat it and start up on plan, it's an easy winner in 2009.

TGR: So, John do you have a prediction on where you think gold will go?

JD: People talk about $2,000 or $5,000—it's all pie in the sky, you know. Gold might get there; but the bigger question is: what's the timeframe? Will I be around when gold is $5,000? I doubt it. Will it get there? Probably.

But we look for undervalued situations no matter what the gold price. And in the '90s—you know we've been writing *Gold Stock Analyst* since 1994—in the mid-90s gold did nothing for three years, it traded between $350 and $400. With our methods of selecting undervalued stocks, we had a couple of years of the Top 10 portfolio up 60% and 70% but gold was flat. Until mid-2008 the GSA Top 10 was up almost 800% in the current gold bull market. When gold does go up, the stocks go up more; but, in general, even if gold does nothing, we can still find good buys. Royal Gold is an example of finding winners in a tough market. Made a Top 10 stock at $23 in mid-2007, it gained 60% in 2008 and has doubled over the past 18 months.

We don't follow the explorers, in part because there is no data to analyze beyond drill hole results, which are a long way from showing a mine can be built and operated at a profit. For us, the pure explorers are too much like lottery tickets. The producers do exploration and you can get your discovery upside from them. Bema Gold (acquired by Kinross Gold in February 2007) was a Top 10 stock with 100,000 ounces per year of production when it found Cerro Casale and it did very nicely on the back of that find. So, with the smaller producers you can get plenty of exploration upside. You don't need to focus on the greenfield explorers because it's just too hard to tell who's going to win and who's going to lose.

John Doody brings a unique perspective to gold stock analysis. With a BA in Economics from Columbia and an MBA in Finance from Boston University, where he also did his Ph.D.-Economics course work, Doody has no formal "rock" studies beyond "Introductory Geology" at Columbia University's School of Mines.

An Economics Professor for almost two decades, Doody became interested in gold due to an innate distrust of politicians. In order to serve those that elected them, politicians always try to get nine slices out of an eight slice pizza. How do they do this? They debase the currency via inflationary economic policies.

Success with his method of finding undervalued gold mining stocks led Doody to leave teaching and start the Gold Stock Analyst newsletter late in 1994. The newsletter covers only producers or near-producers that have an independent feasibility study validating their reserves are economical to produce.

Visit **The GOLD Report** - a unique, free site featuring summaries of articles from major publications, specific recommendations from top worldwide analysts and portfolio managers covering gold stocks, and a directory, with samples, of precious metals newsletters.

The GOLD Report is Copyright by Streetwise Inc. All rights are reserved. Streetwise Inc. hereby grants an unrestricted license to use or disseminate this copyrighted material only in whole (and always including this disclaimer), but never in part. The GOLD Report does not render investment advice and does not endorse or recommend the business, products, services or securities of any company mentioned in this report. From time to time, Streetwise Inc. directors, officers, employees or members of their families, as well as persons interviewed for articles on the site, may have a long or short position in securities mentioned and may make purchases and/or sales of those securities in the open market or otherwise.

ALTERNATIVE INVESTMENTS

And yet another alternative investment: the XAU: A symbol for the Philadelphia Gold and Silver Index, an index of precious metal mining company stocks that are traded on the Philadelphia Stock Exchange.

The Philadelphia Gold and Silver Sector Index (XAU) contain 16 large and medium capitalization weighted companies engaged in the mining of gold and silver. An excellent Index investment, if that's for you.

Van Eck Intl Investors Gold C (IIGCX)

This is a GOLD MUTUAL FUND managed by a geologist. This factor increases value in my opinion. He can spot early-stage gold development companies at good price points. The Van Eck Fund has a solid track record. The expense ratio is generally below 2%. If you're a Gold Mutual Fund investor, consider this option.

THE ART OF INTELLIGENCE

"Impossible only means you haven't found the solution yet." - UNKNOWN

To gain and maintain initiative is based on the military's commander ability to make quick and knowledgeable decisions. The 19th Century military philosopher, Carl von Clausewitz, calls this quick recognition of the truth the commander's *coup d'oeil,* or intuition. It is the ability to recognize the truth, or a high level of awareness, "that the mind would ordinarily miss or would perceive only after long study and reflection." [1]

Clausewitz defines these qualities as "first, an intellect that, even in the darkest hours, retains some glimmering of inner light which leads to truth; second, the courage to follow this faint light wherever it may lead." The first of these qualities is intuition and the second is determination. He further states that the intuition of the genius is not irrational, but it simply reflects a different mode of rationality in which intuitive decisions can be explained ex post facto. Inquisitiveness is a talent of the mind necessary for the proper functioning of intuition.

Another key is that which Voltaire described as the keystone of Marlborough's success – "that calm courage in the midst of tumult, that serenity of soul in danger, which the English call a cool head." That must further be modified by what the French call "le sens du practible" – this is the sense of what is possible versus not possible on a tactical basis. A person must be wise enough to consider an array of details across areas of relevancy.

Planning is the art and science of envisioning a desired future and laying out effective ways of bringing it about. It involves projecting our thoughts forward in time and space so that we can take actions now, *before* they occur, rather than just responding to events after they occur. The consequences of potential actions have to be weighed against the facts. Planning is necessary to reduce the unavoidable time lag between decision and action. *Planning is essential when situations reach a certain level of complexity.* Planning is essential in novel situations in which experience is lacking.

Based on our assessment, we establish goals and objectives we expect to pursue. Then the detail course of action must follow. This involves allocating resources. That is followed by execution of practical measures for carrying out our conceptual planning. Simplicity is not necessarily a virtue in planning – especially if the situation is itself complex.

During and after the execution phase we must be open to changing the plans as we monitor them. To do this we need intelligence sources – raw data which is refined and from which all disinformation is stripped. Adaptability is an utmost consideration – *consider that those who were not adaptable suffered major investment losses* – the old axiom of "buy and hold" just doesn't cut it any more quite obviously.

To think properly we must:

- Look at problems in different ways – find a new perspective.

- Regulate our thinking patterns by requiring new ideas.

- Combine and recombine thoughts in a non-linear fashion.

- Form relationships between what we previously considered dissimilar subjects (oil, geopolitics and war, for example).

- Suspend old forms of what we thought were logic (tenets that are untenable).

- Think in a manner that prepares oneself for multiple outcomes.

- Consider the work of others – through their patience and experience they have developed knowledge that may far exceed ours.

- Think critically – that is, be open-minded.

- Understand the components of risk in our planning.

- Be like Warren Buffet – do not follow the herd, be individualistic and a contrarian investor.

You cannot trust institutional people, as a rule and with certain exceptions, to do your thinking for you. Some of them rely on black-box computer programs relying on complex algorithms and the traders themselves don't have full conception of what the underlying assumptions are. It is estimated that 40% of the trades on the London Stock Exchange are made from black box trading systems. In a contrarian strategy it is believed that all aspects of market behavior revert back to historical averages over time.

Contrarian strategies have now been widely accepted in terms of their ability to deliver superior returns. Gregory, Harris & Michou, in a study some years ago, examined the performance of contrarian strategies in the UK and found that value strategies formed on the basis of a wide range of measures of value have delivered excess returns that are both statistically and economically significant. Under the contrarian model, value strategies are profitable because they are contrarian to naïve strategies such as those that erroneously extrapolate past performance.

Think outside the box. Since the market will enter a bear mode, **use inverse ETFs to hedge your portfolio** if after your due diligence is done you have a green light. Enter the markets carefully after you perform due diligence. Use the right newsletters to aid your efforts. Don't go it all alone. Remember this too – ETFs as a rule operate precisely as they are designed. An inverse ETF tracking the S and P 500 will do the opposite of that index. Some inverse ETFs are structured so as to double that return. They work on a 2X multiplier. If you are certain of your position with a high degree of confidence, then use these.

The Direxion Russell 1000 Financials Bearish 3X ETF (FAZ) is a very powerful option for investors.

This is non-paradigm thinking – remember the key is to do your due diligence, first on the macroeconomics, which you have done by purchasing this book, and then on your allocations as you enter the market.

If you'd like a further resource on the Shadow Government, watch the YouTube video JFK to 911 – Everything is a Rich Man's Trick, produced by a British journalist. It's 3.5 hours long but well worth it.

https://www.youtube.com/watch?v=U1Qt6a-vaNM

[1] Clausewitz, *On War*.

CHINESE DECEPTION

Without the dollar being a reserve currency, the U.S. will sink like a rock.

China has recently announced:

- It is no longer in their interest to accumulate foreign-exchange reserves. Guess what? They are going to stop buying our debt!

- China has new agreements with other nations which exclude the dollar as the basis for the exchange.

- China's central bank is buying gold like it's not going to be available any more!

If no buyers for U.S. debt exist, interest rates can shoot up overnight and that is death to the U.S. stock market. Remember the basic rule of investing: never invest more in any market than you can afford to lose.

In fact, Bloomberg has reported that China recently dumped 50 billion dollars of U.S. debt!

China has to replace this debt with something, and it has chosen gold. Also according to Bloomberg, more than 80% of the gold exports from Switzerland last December went to – guess where – Asia. Chinese gold is imported through Hong Kong.

The average interest rate the U.S. government generously pays on its debt is 2.477%. That is below the inflation rate. What is the advantage of anyone owning these bonds?

But there's more – four large U.S. banks have exposure to derivatives of over 40 trillion dollars. Warren Buffet calls these "financial weapons of mass destruction." With volatility in interest rates there is no way these could be covered.

Let's end with a quote from this article:

> **"Unfortunately, very few of the "experts"**
> **will ever see this crash coming.**
> **Very few of them saw it coming in 2000.**
> **Very few of them saw it coming in 2008.**
> **And very few of them will see it coming this time."**

Source:

Snyder, Michael. "Russia Is Doing It - Russia Is Actually Abandoning The Dollar." The Economic Collapse. Last modified June 10, 2014.

THE END GAME

Now that you've read all of the details behind the planning to implode the U.S. economy, I'll summarize the End Game, as I call it.

The New World Order establishment are the consummate insiders. They know exactly where they are going. Their chief counselors have hidden agendas as well.

In reality, Greenspan is a proponent of gold. The elite's plan all along has been to pump up the fiat money currency to the maximum extent possible, and then let it collapse.

When it collapses it won't be reset in any way we've ever seen. The Federal Reserve is bankrupt and leveraged 77-1. They know they cannot bail it out. Other countries are no longer buying our debt. That won't bail it out.

A couple of Hedge Fund Managers a few years ago came up with an interesting theory. They gamed out the backing of whatever currency remains (I'm talking paper money since stocks will have already been destroyed), and said that if gold was reset at just over $10,000 an ounce that the U.S. paper currency could be gold-backed. I believe the figure is closer to $50,000 an ounce. Since more than 500 currencies not backed by gold or silver have all failed, this of course is the solution.

A devaluation will occur some time after the stock market crash. The market crash will wipe out equities, and the bond market. Banks may close for weeks. The devaluation will be America saying to the world: "Well, we can offer you 20 cents on the dollar." Or whatever formula they use. It'll probably go like this. Well, our debt is half interest anyway. If you all will just forgive that and a little more, we'll be OK to go on with you. Look what's happened here to us anyway. The offer may not be that generous.

American policy since one of our last honest Presidents, Kennedy, has been to put natural resources in protected areas. These protected areas have many names. Environmentally Protected Areas, National Parks and Military Reservations. The Chocolate Mountains of California are an example. They reportedly contain over ten times the gold reserves of Ft. Knox. We've been holding them in reserve for just this type of event. They're guarded by Marines.

The gold in Ft. Knox and the NY Federal Reserve is likely gone, and most likely sold. The government also has the largest oil reserves in the world in Alaska, and they've closed it up pending its use at a time just like this. This has been policy for well over fifty years. They've always known this time is coming, and now it's here.

These hidden natural resources will all become public knowledge shortly after the crash occurs. A lot of chaos will accompany the month of the crash. A batch of Silver American Eagles will be the value of a car.

The "London Silver Fix" ended on August 14, 2014. This was an arrangement by several major banks to "benchmark the price" to their whims.

Now the true price of silver is free to rise to market standards, depending on supply and demand. Silver should trade a minimum 1:1 price ratio with gold. With gold at $1200/ounce, that means silver at $1200/ounce.

The industrial use of silver makes it invaluable in photography, electronics, cells phones, RFID chips and computers and TVs. Silver reflects light and conducts electricity, making it essential in solar panels.

Trillions of dollars from both the West and the East are about to flow into silver as the last monetary haven. The Chinese even have a video produced to their one-billion plus population recommending silver as an investment vehicle. When only a fraction of those billion people buy silver, think of the price demand that will occur.

Silver has the monetary value of gold but on top of this has a multitude of industrial uses. Our paper money is being printed in an out-of-control attempt to prevent the inevitable, which is a banking collapse and derivative meltdown.

I would say that $5000 silver is a conservative estimate. Gold will certainly be in that range soon, but gold doesn't have the price potential of silver.

Less than 1 in 1,000 people will be prepared. It will be the greatest wealth transfer in history. The time to get your house in order is fast closing. Smooth sailing and Godspeed.

In closing, a few of my favorite life quotes:

"Logic will get you from A to Z. Imagination will get you everywhere."
Albert Einstein

"If you think it's expensive to hire a professional to do the job, wait until you hire an amateur."
Red Adair

"Toto, I've a feeling we're not in Kansas anymore."
Dorothy in the Wizard of Oz

David Meade

http://writers-web-services.com

DavidMeade7777@gmail.com

DISCLAIMER

The comments, graphs, forecasts and indices published herein are based upon data whose accuracy is deemed reliable but not guaranteed. Performance returns cited are derived from best estimates. Due diligence is recommended before investing. All investment vehicles contain various measures of risk. This book provides neither legal nor accounting nor investment advice, and disavows any projected results.

BIBLIOGRAPHY

My special thanks to PlanetXNews.com for their allowing me to mirror some of my written articles in Section I.

CPSIA information can be obtained
at www.ICGtesting.com
Printed in the USA
LVHW101343240321
682326LV00012B/624